TEEN-AGERS AND SEX

JAMES A. PIKE

TEEN-AGERS AND SEX

PRENTICE-HALL, INC.
ENGLEWOOD CLIFFS, N.J.

To my teen-age daughter, Connie

Teen-Agers and Sex
by James A. Pike

© 1965 by James A. Pike

Library of Congress Catalog Card Number: 65–25252

Printed in the United States of America
T 90227

PRENTICE-HALL INTERNATIONAL, INC., *London*
PRENTICE-HALL OF AUSTRALIA, PTY., LTD., *Sydney*
PRENTICE-HALL OF CANADA, LTD., *Toronto*
PRENTICE-HALL OF INDIA (PRIVATE) LTD., *New Delhi*
PRENTICE-HALL OF JAPAN, INC., *Tokyo*

FOREWORD

FOR ADULTS ONLY might well have been printed on the dust jacket of this book. Not as a come-on to suggest salaciousness: those seeking pornography would finish these pages in frustration. Not to avoid contributing to the delinquency of minors: there is nothing herein contained that would directly so contribute. Some parental readers may even decide to invite their sons and daughters to read the book or portions of it.

But the book was not written for children or young people. The reasons are these:

1. Without denigrating the role of school and church programs of sex instruction or of books about "the facts of life" for children or teenagers, I am convinced that there is no substitute for direct parental involvement in this impor-

tant aspect of the nurture of children. This book is not meant to fulfill this task for the parents, but to encourage them to undertake it and to assist them in doing so.

2. Two underlying moral theories are operative in our modern society. The choice as to whether to promote one or the other (or to present them as alternatives, recognizing that the youth may be grounding his thinking or acting on a theory different from that of his elders), should be the parents', not the author's. The aim here is to help parents best present the facts and implications within the approach chosen. While a large proportion of parents are quite definite in their ethical views (whether conservative or liberal) regarding premarital sex, many, many parents are frankly bewildered and are inconsistent or immobilized in their guidance function. Until such parents think clearly about the problem, they can be of little help to their children. Hence, the direction of this volume to parents.

3. Writing for parents enables me to be fully candid at an adult level of language. I realize that parents will be selecting what they sense is appropriate for their own children at particular ages and will "translate" what is selected (plus other ideas, of course) into suitable terms.

In the writing I have had in mind principally the needs of fathers and mothers; hence I have used the

word "parent" in almost every instance where desig-
nating the instructor/counselor. But actually there are
many others professionally involved in communication to and counseling of young people in this area,
e.g., priests, ministers, rabbis and physicians, school
counselors and teachers; guidance officers, and others.
I hope this volume will be of some use to many of
them, yet I could think of no single generic word em-
bracing parents and these other categories of helpful
persons. Hence, I will simply assume that any of the
latter reading these pages will substitute his own professional designation for the word "parent" in all applicable places.

I anticipate that in response to this book, as in the
case of others I have written in the fields of personal
anxiety and social ethics, many will say that most of it
doesn't seem particularly "religious." But religion has
to do with concern for the whole of life and experience,
and no religious tradition (including my own Angli-
can heritage) has already "packaged" viable answers
—catechism-fashion—for all of the questions and
searchings-out in this realm (or in any other, I might
add). World-view and premises, yes—and these have
been set forth (I hope with some adequacy) in this
book; but extensive analysis and the manifold applica-
tions, no. Yet the concern is most certainly within the
realm of religion—if the latter be not too narrowly
conceived. For the author, and I hope for many of the
parents and young people, the conclusions are formed
by a religious perspective.

In closing I would like, as is customary and appropriate, to acknowledge those who have helped most. But since most of my practical understanding of this realm of human life has come from a multitude of occasions of pastoral counseling for over twenty years, I cannot remember in most instances who added to my insights in this or that particular. Even when my memory has served me in this regard, the proper restriction of confidentiality inherent in the pastoral relation would bar my revealing names, even in the desire to give credit to many who have enabled me, hopefully, to be of help at this point to many more people and their children. But if any of counselees recognize situations presented to me at one time or another, they can regard themselves as thanked most appreciatively. I am able to give explicit thanks to my own four children who have listened, asked good questions and shared with me their thoughts and those of their peer groups. I wish to express my thanks to my wife, Esther, with whom—naturally—I have over the years talked about most of this subject matter; and to the office secretarial staff and others for patient work in the preparation of the typescript. I appreciate also the assistance of Mary K. Jones, educational consultant of the Diocese of California, responsible for a diocesan program of instruction in this field for parents and teen-agers, who reviewed the manuscript, and contributed the last half of Chapter 4. Thanks are due to my chaplain, the Rev. David Baar, B.D., who prepared the annotated bibliography; and Mr. Stuart L. Daniels, whose analysis of the manuscript was most constructive. Also I have appreciated the opportunity to "try out" discussion of this subject at Barnard and Radcliffe Colleges, at the University of California and at Foothill College, to whose authorities I express my gratitude.

Should this effort take the form of a second edition, I trust that the foreword for it will include many more acknowledgments, since I hope for—indeed solicit— criticisms and sharing of experience by parents and other counselors. In any case, whether I hear about it or not, I pray (and I mean this in a literal sense) that through this effort, principally mediated through concerned adults, many young people may receive some light for their efforts at responsible decision making through particularly happy/trying years and be helped toward maturity not only during the teens, but in all the years of their lives.

✠ JAMES A. PIKE

The Cathedral Close
San Francisco
Michaelmas, 1965

CONTENTS

Foreword   v

1   A New Challenge to Parents   1
2   Conflicting Currents   16
3   The Meaning of Sexual Intercourse   33
4   When and How to Talk   39
5   The First Phase   54
6   The Second Phase   62
7   The Third Phase   77
8   Emotional Involvement   92
9   Alcohol and Sex   112
10   Toward Marriage   127
Bibliography   141

TEEN-AGERS AND SEX

1 ♒

A NEW CHALLENGE
TO PARENTS

We are in the midst of a sexual revolution—a revolution which in some measure affects people of all ages and localities. To say this is almost commonplace today. But not as generally understood is the bearing this has on what parents ought to tell their children, especially before and during their teens. For many decades enlightened parents have recognized that one of their most important responsibilities toward their young people is instruction about sex. The quality of this instruction has, like anything else, been good, bad or indifferent. Now the whole matter of approach needs reexamination in the light of the change in the general milieu. The purpose of this book is to offer guidance to parents about the best way to fulfill this task in our times. First, we will examine what the present situation is in our everyday life in contrast to older patterns. Then we will take a critical look at what has been the typical approach to sex instruction. From that point we shall be ready to consider an approach which may be more fruitful in meeting the present day needs of young people and their likely needs in the years ahead.

THE NATURE OF THE SEXUAL REVOLUTION

There is obviously nothing new about sex as such; nor are unconventional sexual behavior and the problems associated with it simply characteristic of the time in which we live. It is only in recent times that statistical studies in this field have been available; so it is difficult to make comparisons. But the greater the knowledge of the mores of various generations of various cultures, the more obvious it is that in all times and places there has been a considerable degree of nonconformity with the taken-for-granted mores. It is evident that there is little basis for nostalgic reference to "the good old days" when people are supposed to have "behaved." Yet, taking into account the decades in which more or less indicative surveys have been made, it is true that there has been a rapid increase in "nonconformity" with accepted standards of sexual expression on the part of persons of all ages.

But a much more important change has been occurring. In our culture in the past, those who deviated from the established mores generally thought they were sinning—and certainly the conformists thought that they were. Now we are living in a time when there is widespread questioning, indeed outright challenging, of conventional standards. In the minds of

2

many people, young and old, there is increasing doubt as to what constitutes sin or goodness in this realm; and on the part of quite a few there is outright rejection of the category of sin.

This new challenge is not only from pornographic quarters. Scholars in the social sciences, and other spokesmen, have articulated doubts and rejections. Such doubts have existed even among the clergy for some time—in the past usually articulated only in pastoral counseling, but now being expressed openly in sermons and writings. There is increasing friction on this question in our culture. Meanwhile, the doubters and the challengers are fast achieving the status of respectability—academic and otherwise.

The turmoil in this field is reflected not only in learned journals, but in textbooks on morals; not only in sleazy paperbacks, but in widely acclaimed novels. To these almost everybody has access, including our young people; so it is ostrichlike for parents to ignore the fact as they assess their role of instruction and influence. Whatever one's personal view on this fundamental question, all would agree that there is considerable difference between a person's saying, "Okay, it's wrong; but I'm going to do it," and saying, "It's not wrong."

This book is not intended as a text on moral theology or ethics.* Here we will candidly recognize that two

* The author has not dodged this area of discourse: see *A Time for Christian Candor* (New York: Harper & Row, 1964), ch. 5, and *Doing the Truth* (New York: Macmillan, rev. ed., 1965), ch. 13.

or more points of view exist, and we will seek to articulate and interpret them. Outlined will be a program for instruction for teen-agers which takes into account the existence of these views and their likely impact upon our young people. The actual application of what is here said will vary on the part of given parent-counselors, depending on their own view of the matter. But as we shall see, the point of view of the parent is not necessarily the determinative factor in actual conduct. So any sensible plan of instruction and guidance, whatever the particular mentor's point of view, should take into account the fact that today in our culture there is not simply one set of convictions about the matter.

The sexual revolution is not the only factor that makes the task of the parent more complex. Other things have been happening too. Following are some of them.

THE CHANGING HOME PATTERN

There is no question that familial ties are rapidly weakening. With the increase of distractive activities, members of a family spend much less time together than in past decades. For example, increasingly infrequent is the family meal encompassing all its members (usually two or three times a day, day in and day out, week in and week out). Generally now adults and young people alike get their own breakfasts, when it is most convenient for each. Lunch is rarely eaten at home. As for dinner, sometimes one or both parents are out, and the respective children have their own plans which seem to prevent them from sitting down at the table at some fixed hour with everybody "reporting in" together. For evenings and weekends, and vacations too, more often than not the respective members of the family go their own way—not only out of the house, but in the house—one or two at the TV, one or two studying, one or two with friends, one or two asleep or what not.

Two other familial factors should be mentioned. With the enhanced role of women, there is less often a single authority figure in the home. Also, with the increasing amount of separation and divorce, for the parent without custody there is often a limited opportunity for influence.

THE INCREASING INDEPENDENCE OF YOUTH

Increasingly rare is the home in which there is marked deference and respect for the parents on the part of children and teen-agers. Not only is there more "talking back," but there is decreasing discipline in response thereto. There is more independent thinking —sound or unsound—and more articulation of it. Wrongly or rightly, young people have much less fear of pursuing their own bent, whether or not it meets with parental approval. One striking example: There was a day when a father's approval of a fiancé was a condition *sine qua non* to a marriage. Now "asking her father's consent" is almost quaint, and if the

5

ritual is gone though both the suppliant and the father are generally quite well aware that a "No" will not be conclusive as to the outcome; this often affects the process of answering the ceremonial question. As for family plans, once when parents (or perhaps the father!) decided what the family would do as a group, either at home or on an outing or on vacation, there was little question that all would participate. Now young people are not very hesitant about announcing frankly (sometimes kindly) that they are having no part of it. And on fundamental questions, such as sex ethics, teenagers these days do not hesitate to admit openly that they do not agree with their parents' standards and have no particular intention of following them.

OUTSIDE INFLUENCES

Along with these other factors is the increasing influence of nonfamilial factors on our young people. John Donne's centuries-old dictum, "No man is an island entire of itself" holds. No young person is "on his own" when he forms his standards or makes his decisions; and hence as the family influence weakens, other influences strengthen. A decrease of parental contact does not necessarily mean more aloneness on the part of our young people; they simply spend more time with others outside the home. Particularly influential are the attitudes found among their contemporaries or peer group. "What everybody does," "Keep-up with the Joneses," fear of what "they say"—all this is age-old; but generally for the parents this had been an influence (again, sound and unsound) toward conformity. Now, for our young people what these phrases represent is still an influence toward conformity with the peer group—which may well mean *non*conformity with conventional ethics.

Further, increasing freedom from censorship has made available to our young people candid treatments of sex. They see many works (principally paperback) which are loaded on the side of sexual freedom, and some of which directly seek to make a case against traditional restraints. Much they see and hear in films, on television and from popular records, glorifies sexual experience, or, at the least, inculcates a lighthearted, accepting attitude toward nonconformity. Further, television especially (since it now occupies more of young people's time) is effective in inculcating a more global outlook of man's ways, reducing "taken-for-grantedness" of mores in this field, as in others.

Thus young people are influenced by the words and behavior of those other than their parents—and by the parents' actual behavior (in contrast to the parents' words). And they are likely to be particularly insensitive to the factor of maturity, which is a valid one, in distinguishing juvenile choices from adult choices. What they see around them and hear freely would suggest that things are "all right" which their parents and the Church have said are wrong. To a degree such factors have existed in all generations; but our young people today are more aware of them; they are allowed

7

to see more, hear more. The hope that all this can be kept from them, by specific restraints in the household or by a sterner public censorship, is probably a lost cause.

THE PSYCHOLOGICAL AGE

In times past (and perhaps among naïve parents today) this whole subject has been viewed as simply a matter of morals and discipline. Children are to be taught the right thing and they are to do it, or be made to do it, or suffer explicit penalties for not doing it. Today parents who think or read at all are increasingly insecure, and confused, about their role. Whether or not they are "semi-pros" in depth psychology in general, or in child psychology in particular, they have become increasingly fearful of dogmatism, repression and forms of discipline. They may fear unconventional behavior on the part of their young people; but they fear as much the possible aftereffects, in years ahead, of approaches too patterned and disciplines too stern.

Further, as is the increasingly prevalent pattern in regard to adult behavior, they tend to view deviation not so much as a simple sin or fault, but as the outcome of familial, social and psychological factors. More and more often the question is not "What did he do?" but "Why did he do it?"

Parents tend to carry quite a load of guilt (often

8

unwarranted) about the children's behavior, fearful either that they have not held the reins tightly enough or that they have held them too tightly. Because of this confusion and uncertainty, in an age of transition between two quite different approaches to life and human personality, they are literally "stumped" on particular occasions. The result is hesitation and inconsistency in reaction. Our young people are increasingly aware of this fact—and less is their "repentance." Often they manifest indifference or provide explanations—however immaturely put—in terms of supposed or real traumata in earlier years, or supposed or real social conditioning, or supposed or real effects of present parental attitudes. Particularly baffling to a parent is a young person who is unwilling to enter (or who is perhaps incapable of entering) into discourse on such matters on an ethical level at all.

The effects upon most of our youth today are composite, e.g., the Church, the parent and the "official" mores on one side, the peer group, paperbacks, mass media, etc., on the other. But with some, parental influences register zero, and other influences add up to 100 percent. As this process develops, the parents are aware of an increasing alienation (though sometimes not without courteous expression). They find that talk and more talk has no effect and that discipline (even of a very restrictive sort) does not change inner attitudes—or, for that matter, outward behavior—entirely (there seem always to be ways 'round). Indeed they may be aware that the talking and the discipline are increasing the alienation. And their worries move from the moral realm to the psychological one.

WIDER KNOWLEDGE

There was a time when parental instruction represented the first real knowledge of sex gained by young people. I was fortunate to have been instructed at the appropriate ages on different aspects of the matter, and I recall that I came to these moments with only scattered and fragmentary impressions gained from *sotto voce* conversations with little friends. But today young people are quite well-informed, and they will have learned a lot about sex, with varying degrees of soundness and/or distortion, whether we talk to them or not. In the past just because children were generally uninformed, more sophisticated parents tended to approach the matter quite obliquely in order not to surprise or shock, and sometimes because of fear of creating negatives in the process of laying the foundation for sound thought and behavior. This is not so great a risk today unless the timing of conversation about the subject is premature. Generally, the youngster comes with a great deal of knowledge (much of it true) hiding in his head. They tell of one parent who had covered reproduction among the birds and the bees, only to have the child exclaim, "Oh, just like people!" The change is at least a time-saver! Often it would seem best now to get right to the subject. (If the parents wishes to increase the extent of the child's zoological learning, he may *add* that all this is true of other mammals and, in a measure, of other creatures as well.)

INCREASING MOBILITY

First, for a long time there has been greater availability of means of transportation, particularly the automobile (it has become almost impossible to deny young people the use of the latter). Thus our young people get around easily and are relatively freer to carry through with their own plans and those of their "gang" or "crowd" out of the reach of the parental eye. And, openly or in secret, they are much freer to engage in drinking or in sexual activity apart from past accustomed controls.

Second, there is another type of mobility which affects the situation. Once families usually stayed in the same house on the same street in the same community for years. There societal factors of influence and restraint could be counted upon, at least in a measure, unless the youngster simply "broke the traces." But now more and more of our families move from house to house, town to town, state to state, with increasing rapidity; and young people are thrown into varying patterns year after year. And with this there is increasing indifference on their part (as indeed there is on the part of the parents) as to what the people around them may think.

While everywhere there is a definite movement

toward greater freedom in sexual attitudes, the general drift of one community can differ markedly from that of another. Yet they are at different levels on the same escalator (I leave the reader to decide whether it should be regarded as the up-escalator or the down-escalator!). I have talked to parents in various parts of the country and find that in more settled and stable communities, where people tend to stay awhile, there is considerably more conservatism in the attitudes and activities on the part of the young people; and—unless the parents in such communities whom I have spoken to have their heads totally in the sand—there are at present fewer menacing problems for the parents. In other communities, in even the most respectable areas, being "way out" is fast becoming accepted in the peer group, and parents tend to feel that they are fighting a losing battle—if they are fighting at all. The *trend*, however, seems to be the same in all localities. It seems simply to be a matter of time. Hence, parents in what are presumed to be the more conservative areas might well want to anticipate how things are heading even there, and take this into account in the scope and mode of their conversations with young people on the subject.

INCREASING FOCUS ON SEX

Human attitudes and actions are like a long complex mural on a wall; the actual influences and attitudes depend upon how the lighting is placed. Never does everything receive equal emphasis. There are no new factors in human life, but there is no question that the "lighting" these days is focused more sharply on the sexual aspect of existence—an area in the mural of life which in the past was left in darkness or dim light. That wasn't particularly healthy, either, and we do not wish to return to such times. In any case, we can't. Well might we wish that the lighting on sex were somewhat modified, at least in proportion to the many other realities and possibilities in life. The fact is that we are living in the age we are in, and no one family can turn back the clock.

Some young people today have great preoccupation with time-filling hobbies, sports and conventional group activities. But many couldn't care less for these things, or regard them as secondary to interest in the opposite sex—expressed sexually or not. Boys who in times past might have been concentrating on becoming Eagle Scouts are today spending more time and thought on "making out" with girls, "booming around" in souped-up cars, or "hanging around" with the gang. Quickly organized (generally disorganized!) impromptu activities more and more are the order of the day (and night) rather than scheduled programs.

Most of us now recognize that for centuries suppression of sexual thoughts and impulses did damage to people's ongoing emotional life. At the same time we see damage of a different type threatened by the predominance of the sexual motif in the lives of an increasing number of our young people, and its predominance in the very air they breathe—and we breathe. Obviously, the pendulum has swung too rapidly from one extreme to the other. Most of us know that silence and a "naughty, naughty" approach are no longer possible; yet few of us are willing to endorse the other extreme. Still we are not quite sure where the middle is, or if we do think we know where it is, we find it difficult to articulate it in a plausible and convincing manner to the next generation.

CHANGE IN PEDAGOGICAL METHODS

This book is not the place to discuss various theories of education, all the way from indoctrination and learning propositions by rote to permissiveness centered around the individual response of the moment. But the fact is that for the past three or four decades there has been a considerable shift in educational methodology on the part of the principal educative instrumentalities in our society. In schools and in youth groups there is a decrease of indoctrinating and teaching of "principles," and an increase in using the person-centered method. This is true of the Church as well, though in some denominations there has been a lagging behind the trend. As a result, parental instruction in this realm—or in any other—simply in terms of principles and rules which are stated as universal and self-authenticating, is out of step with methodologies otherwise brought to bear upon one's sons and daughters. Whether or not this incongruity is consciously noted by the child, the parent is apt to lose out in the competition, and what is said turns out to be less and less influential, if indeed it does not seem irrelevant. To use an increasingly employed semantic distinction, the young people may hear, but they do not necessarily "hear"—a modern version of the old phrase "in one ear and out the other."

A summary of these factors, and there are others, is not meant to add up to the conclusion that parents do not have a role here. If that were the case this would be not only the first, but also the last chapter of this book. On the contrary, the parental role is not less; it is greater, but it is more difficult by far. The fact is that for most young people today the once typical "sex talk" is not harmful; but it will doubtless not be very useful. (How useful it was in previous decades we have no accurate way of measuring.) When a parent is realistic about what he is confronting (whatever his own ethical system may be) and applies wisdom, thought and active sensitivity in discharging his task, he can play an important role indeed. It is his responsibility to seek to do so.

2 ✍✍

CONFLICTING
CURRENTS

An ideal beach for ocean swimming is one where the waves come in with moderate force and the waters return with milder force and little undertow. More expertise and caution is called for where the undertow is stronger or where, on a rocky shore, strong waves are thrown back against the incoming currents.

Doubtless there are communities—or even individual families—sufficiently isolated and self-protected that the current of conventional sexual morality is comparable to the first aquatic description. But in most places the undertow is increasing in force; and, in many, two sets of waves are in sharp concussion, creating a confusion of the waters.

The consequent parental task might be somewhat easier if the conflict of currents affected only young people. But this is not something going on in a wading-pool for children; adults too are caught up in it. It is not simply that all those of our generation know the answers and are only concerned with communicating them adequately and persuasively to our children.

Many adults are not sure of the answers themselves; so, to use a Biblical image, the trumpet gives out an uncertain sound. In any case, whatever the parental view, the fact that there are two directions of sexual morality must be faced as the parent seeks to discharge his task of guidance. Before going further we should outline the two principal views, keeping in mind especially their different underlying premises as well as their varying consequences.

THE CONVENTIONAL VIEW

The word "conventional" is not meant in a derogatory sense. I almost used the word "traditional" but realized its inaccuracy: what tradition in what culture in what period? What I mean by "conventional" is the view which until recently has been generally taken for granted in our society: an explicit set of standards without "respectable" challenge. As has been indicated, we must distinguish this view from actual *conduct* in the past. What we are talking about is what our society has been saying is "right," and from which deviation has been almost universally labeled as "sin."

This view expresses itself in simple formulae: Sexual intercourse is wrong except in marriage. Masturbation is wrong *per se*. Sexual contact between persons of the same sex is wrong *per se*. Sexual contact—short of intercourse—between persons of the opposite sex is wrong when it passes a particular line (as to just where this line is there is less definiteness than in the previous statements).

17

Why are these things wrong? Here a variety of supports ranging from absolutism to pragmatism come into play. Some simply believe "it is wrong because it is wrong." Some will refer to "God's will" or "the teaching of the Church." Some who are more Bible-centered will say that "the Bible teaches that it is wrong." While, taking the Bible as a whole, there are portrayed, sometimes endorsively or uncritically, what many today would regard as unconventional sexual arrangements, there are any number of texts which express a prohibition of sex apart from the marriage bed. Some, especially those raised in the Roman Catholic Church will ground the prohibition in the "natural law." One theory is that the primary function, and *only* primary function, of sexual activity is procreation, an outcome suitable only for married couples. Others who would include a second primary function, namely, the expression and nourishing of the love of two persons for one another, would assert that as a matter of immutable principle such expression and nourishment of love is appropriate only for a man and a woman who have committed themselves to each other for life, "for better for worse, for richer for poorer, in sickness and in health. . . ." Total giving and receiving sexually is seen as right only where, by virtue of marriage, there is total sharing and responsibility one for another on all levels.

Moving from this absolutist base, many ground their negative conviction in "the standards of society." Some (innocent of studies in anthropology or comparative culture) will assert that everybody, everywhere, has believed that the specified forms of conduct are wrong. Or there will be a shift to a norm of esthetics: "it's not nice," "it's nasty, unclean." Or reference is made to the bearing on "character": "it's cheap," "no nice girl does it," "only bad people do these things." Or, moving somewhat more toward the pragmatic approach: "People won't respect you." Or, moving to a frankly pragmatic base (either as the principal argument or a supportive argument), there are dangerous consequences: pregnancy, disease, scandal.

Strictures against sexual expressions short of intercourse also have a variety of supports. Sometimes these are grounded in absolute statements about specific sins. Sometimes there is a pragmatic approach based on the obvious fact that certain contacts do indeed stir the emotions and lead to more complete contacts and often to intercourse itself. Sometimes this approach is supplemented by explicit instruction as to type and duration of kisses and of manual contacts.

Let us assume that the conventional view is the right one and that the given parent has no question about it. The fact is that if instruction is limited to "playing a record" about the conventional moral standards the results are likely to be less than rewarding, for the following reasons.

QUESTIONING OF ABSOLUTES

We live in a day when people—young and old—do not necessarily accept absolutes without question. Thus flat assertions that such-and-such is sin (whether because of the Church, the Bible, or "natural law") is apt to sound rather hollow. In times past, for a large proportion of young people, the mere fact that the parents or other respected adults said that X is true, was sufficient. But as has been suggested earlier, the parent is no longer as successful as an authority-figure (and, incidentally, as we have learned from psychiatry, such success may have been at a pretty high price). The fact is that our young people are hearing other voices. Their increasing tendency to listen to other voices is enhanced by natural and wholesome developments during puberty and adolescence, when their emotions are in conflict with their learned "principles." They are sitting ducks for the process of rationalization, a process which actively works to minimize negatives. And, as also has been suggested earlier, with their decreasing respect for parental tutelage, there is increasing exaltation of the attitudes of the peer group. In all times nonconformity with respect to one's peers is reticently engaged in. But now in sex morals what was once nonconformity is becoming conformity.

Thus it would appear superficially that our *pragmatic* arguments would be of greater force in encouraging our young people to "toe the mark." It may well be that more adults than young people know that the ground has shifted under some of these pragmatic arguments; but my experience would indicate that young people are rapidly catching on, too. Let us assess these arguments one by one in terms of their current degree of persuasiveness.

Risks to reputation This argument certainly had

great weight in times past—at least to the female in
our culture. We are not entirely sure (because of the
"double standard") that it ever represented a devastat-
ing negative as far as males were concerned. Now
the question is whether, pragmatically speaking, it *is*
a negative. Much as some may regret it, many of our
young people are not particularly "put off," in terms
of choice of mate, or of a fiancé, by the other's previous
sexual experience. Nor are their friends and acquaint-
ances of the same sex necessarily "put off." They may
actually share the standards of the unconventional
acquaintance. Or they may display what is an ever
widening tolerance in regard to all aspects of behavior.
They may simply say, "Well, that's the way he looks
at it" or "That's the way she lives her life." In fact,
in many circles reputation for sexual activity may enhance the status of a person. There is increasing conviction on the part of many females that an experienced sexual partner is an asset—either for dating or
for marriage itself. And to a lesser extent—but to a
growing extent—the converse is true: "She knows
her way around," "She is experienced in bed," is not
necessarily a complete "write-off" of the girl in question. Even where it does express a minus judgment,
sometimes mixed with that judgment is the declaration of a plus. Although many would view this state of
things as unfortunate, it would not appear that our
culture is moving away from this attitude. Rather, it
would seem to be moving more and more in that
direction. In the light of all this, fewer of our young

people are worried about their "reputations" as they make their decisions in this realm.

Danger of pregnancy   This is not a new phenomenon among the unmarried, but the attitude toward it has certainly changed. It used to be the greatest shame that could befall a family; now more often it is taken in stride. There is greater charity in the newer attitude; and at the same time there has been a proportionate reduction in the deterrent element. And this at a time when there is much more widespread knowledge among young people (as a generation ago there was among adults) concerning contraceptive methods. Young people who have decided to "go ahead" are not at all eager to produce offspring and quite often they "use their heads."

In the old days contraception was assumed to be a male responsibility, the boy practicing *coitus interruptus* or *coitus reservatus* or coming equipped with condoms. Now girls are beginning more and more to assume responsibility: carrying condoms in their purses or managing to have been fitted with a diaphragm, or, according to a recent trend increasingly widely reported, putting themselves on a regular schedule of contraceptive pills. How the appropriate equipment is obtained need not concern us here; the fact is that it is obtainable and used very widely. All this tends to weaken the pragmatic argument of the threat of pregnancy.

It is true that none of these methods are totally certain and that risk cannot be totally eliminated. But this argument is not conclusive to many young people today. For a large number of them, risk in life is taken for granted. (This is true of young people and adults alike, especially in the nuclear age, when hanging over all is an overall "if" as to the future.) Even the more responsible ones may be content with the fact that there is a fairly high degree of protection afforded by contraception. And there *is*, as a matter of fact—depending of course on which method is adopted and how consistently it is utilized.

Danger of infection   In past decades, this fear was often assuaged by the use of condoms or of easily-purchased prophylactics to be used after intercourse. But always there was the grievous and well-grounded fear that *if* infection occurred, the consequences were very deleterious and, in the case of syphilis, perhaps lifelong. But, as most adults now know, with the almost 100 percent effective treatment available, medical science has minimized considerably the consequences that need ensue. Many young people know this too; and if anything, they are overly casual about the likelihood of any consequences worth worrying about.

Fear of scandal   This goes back to the matter of reputation and also involves the fear of particular social consequences, such as dismissal from school or the loss of parental favor. But here, too, the times have changed; our young people are given much more freedom to move about unchaperoned and "on their own wheels" and as a result there is a much wider variety of opportunity for effecting sexual relationships under discreet circumstances. Even those young people who might feel that their reputation would be lost were their activities known, can be reasonably sure that with sufficient care their activities will not be known.

In summary, the role some of these negatives played in the past has changed. Then the line was drawn—and wisely enough—at a given point because of "conception, infection and detection," but the situation has changed in regard to each of these. Though these threats are not out of the picture, in the minds of many young people instead of being supports for a "No" answer, they are recognized and dealt with in connection with a "Yes" answer. Will they be sensible enough to recognize that they might "get caught" anyway? The answer to this is likely to be one of the following: "I'm using my head so as not to get caught," or "Maybe so, but that's a chance I'll take—like crossing the street or traveling by air." Our own behavior as parents in this modern world certainly does not set an example of absolute unwillingness to take risks; we are doing it all the time. And at no time in history have youth, by and large, been more conservative about risks than mature adults.

Present vs. future There is one remaining argument which has often been used by parents and which is a mixture of principle and pragmatism: sex is something to be saved for one's lifelong partner; if it is engaged in now something will be lost for the long-run. Regardless of how valid or invalid this may be in terms of personality development, there is little we can put before our young people, in terms of empirical data, about what matters will be like (with or without previous sex) that would be very convincing—except our own say-so. Furthermore, this say-so would have to be said by many present-day parents with tongue-in-cheek (either consciously or unconsciously); even among adults a high proportion of males and a fairly considerable proportion of females have had sexual experience prior to marriage. Many of these may not really regret it or feel that it damaged their marriage. If the marriage is happy they will probably not give great weight to the effect of premarital experience, and if the marriage is unhappy, they will probably not attribute the difficulty precisely to the fact that one or another of the partners had been sexually involved before marriage.

But even if the parental instructor is logically or experientially convinced of the point, in the present climate of opinion it is not likely to score very high with the pupil. Youth has always approached life existentially in terms of the "here-and-now" (another pizza though a stomachache likely later). This is more and more true of our young people today. It is increasingly difficult, for example, to keep young people at their homework with arguments about their future success in a career, or to persuade them to take it easy today and tonight so that they will be refreshed for an examination tomorrow, or to induce them to save money in high school in order to have more spending money in college. (We adults are not always very reliable in this regard either!)

To go back to the precise point, actually an increasing number of our young people are putting a premium on sexual experience now, having heard somewhere that it better prepares them for marriage. They may even have picked up the notion that sexual intimacy is one way to increase love and commitment to a given person with whom they would like to be engaged, or married, or simply "going steady." How much of this is fact and how much of it is rationalization is not the question here. The fact is that such analyses do have their place in youthful thinking (and sometimes in the thinking of adults).

EFFECT OF PARENTS' VIEW

Throughout the foregoing discussion I have been assuming that the parent really holds to the conventional view and wishes successfully to "sell it" to his children. The attempt at realism is not meant as a series of arguments against the heretofore accepted absolute code. What we are talking about is the likely effectiveness of a pedagogical process, and it is in this spirit that I address myself to a concluding point about the conventional approach in instruction. Merely declaring what the moral law is and telling them to observe it, will have very little bearing on the actual conduct of young people. Give it to them "straight" if you wish, but do not have too high a level of expectancy as to the results. If this makes you feel insecure as a parent in relation to your children, then that is your problem and not directly theirs. (Incidentally, your insecurity in this regard is *indirectly* their problem, but it is one broader than the scope of the subject at hand.) In any case, you can console yourself somewhat by the fact that if your children goose-step to your commands, it is likely that you have been doing them damage in another way which may have lifelong deleterious effects; you probably don't want it that way, either.

On the other hand, this does not mean that your attitudes and example will have no effect, or should have no effect. What you are as a person, the way your life has seemed to work out, will have a bearing—if you have earned the respect of your children. More than that, the various *factors* which you mention in discussion may well find a place in the weighing they do. But in the end many youths, perhaps the more healthy-minded of them, will do their own weighing. And be prepared for the possibility that they may read the scales differently from you.

Now we turn to what in our culture is a newer (but not, for this reason, better) approach to sexual ethics.

"THE NEW MORALITY"

This is a label, given first by a papal encyclical opposed to it, to an ethical school of thought. It should not be confused with the case for a "free" sexual ethic which is becoming increasingly articulate. "The New Morality" rests on premises broader than sexual ethics; they come down to something like this: God as the one Absolute is the Source of an absolute claim upon man to make each decision responsibly. Except for this there are no absolutes. Codes of conduct are not universal; they are part of historical development and social conditioning. Each particular ethical decision stands on its own footing and should take into account all the discernible factors found in the given context. For this reason the approach is sometimes called "situational ethics" (a phrase also applied first by a Pope). It is part of the general outlook on life known as *existentialism*.

Applied to sexual ethics this approach would replace an absolute Yes or an absolute No, inside or outside marriage, with a requirement of responsible decision-making in regard to each specific relationship at the given time and in the context of the various significant relative factors. First to be evaluated would be the quality of the one-to-one relationship itself. The question would be: Is the personal tie of sufficient depth to make appropriate its expression and its fueling by a given degree of erotic sharing? Inherent in this question is a prior one: What extent of intimacy is appropriate or what measure of personal involvement and commitment? Then, if the answer to these two questions conjoined is some form of Yes, other questions follow: What would be the likely ongoing effect on each of the partners, especially in a situation without societal structure? If in the picture are spouses or others to whom there are varying degrees of involvement or commitment, what would be the likely effect of the given Yes on these ongoing relationships and, perhaps, responsibilities? Etc. The very raising of such questions demonstrates that the approach is one of responsibility, but with the conviction that answers taking into account the claims of both fulfillment and responsibility will not be found in a Code, but through an analysis of specific situations, which come in many, many different configurations.

Many of my readers will be flatly opposed to such notions. Others may not be opposed to existentialism in general but yet be opposed to its application to the field of sexual morality. Yet if they would prepare themselves for the task with which this book is concerned, it is important that they not write off this point of view as something which will never touch the thinking of their young people. Nor should they simply "lump" it with immorality and irresponsibility.

Actually, such a point of view would deem itself ethical and responsible, recognizing the fact that the exercise of responsibility under such an outlook is a much more difficult task than a judgment made on a basis of a flat absolute code. And whether we generally take an absolutist view of ethics or an existentialist one, all of us are accustomed to making somewhat complex, "iffy," decisions in many matters. No moral code devised in any culture has been adequate to cover the whole range of human decision making. More often than not, particularly in regard to more serious matters, we are engaged in the task of balancing projected goods and evils (taking account of the likelihood of differing effects on different persons concerned). For example: The Roman Catholic Church is generally thought to have an absolute code of ethics. Yet a given Roman Catholic couple's decision to use or not to use the rhythm method at a given period in their married life does not involve the automatic application of a clear law. Rather it involves the responsible weighing of the factors in a given context—just as responsible family planning on the part of persons of other religious traditions requires such weighing as to use of medically approved contraceptives. This same kind of ethical weighing enters into the decision as to whether to dismiss a certain employee for the possible greater good of the company. The same is true of the necessity forced upon some couples to decide whether separation and/or divorce is best. Many choices involve a decision as to the best use (in a sense of stewardship under God) of one's talents and means and time. We just don't have "rule-book" answers for all these questions as they come up in individual lives. (Likewise this is true in forming a responsible view on public questions. For example, when is war right? The pacifist, on the one hand, or the "jingoist," on the other hand, has an easier time here than most of us.)

Though it would appear that as to sex ethics there is a distinct cleavage between absolutists and existentialists, in application there actually is not. A believer in "situational ethics" would weigh *factors* for his decision just as an absolutist would regard *arguments* for his position. In terms of actual implementation the answers might well come out the same in many instances. Certainly Christian writers who have adopted an existentialist premise place considerable emphasis on factors which would lead in many cases to a negative decision.*

In fact the parental counselor who himself adopts the absolutist view and yet fears that his son or daughter may veer to a more existentialist approach will find that if he has communicated the bases of his position well, he has not wasted his breath. What for him were bases for an absolute position may be taken by his hearer as significant factors to weigh in a situational decision. And the reverse may happen. Not infrequently today, the parent has shifted to a situational outlook on ethics while the son or daughter endorses the conventional view. Mention by existentialist parrents of factors which are to be weighed may well be taken by the young person as convincing arguments for an absolute No. Whatever the views of the parent or of the child, the fact is that there are two strong currents in our culture and any realistic counseling should take both into account. Their existence will be reflected in the pages that follow. But there is still a matter more fundamental than either of these basic views—namely, the way actual intercourse itself is to

* E.g., H. A. Williams, Dean of Trinity College, Cambridge, in *Soundings*, ed. A. Vidler (Cambridge: Cambridge University Press, 1962), pp. 81–82; *Towards a Christian View of Sex*, ed. Haron (Friends Home Service Comm., 1963); J. A. T. Robinson, *Honest to God* (London: S.C.M.; Philadelphia: Westminster, 1963); Robinson, *Christian Morals Today* (London: S.C.M., 1964); Canon Douglas Rhymes (of Southwark Cathedral), *No New Morality* (London: Constable, Philadelphia: Westminster, 1964), and from my, *Doing The Truth*.

be understood and interpreted to those for whom we have responsibility and whom we would counsel. In the long run, even more fundamental than what precisely our sons and daughters will and will not do is what they understand to be the meaning of the sex act itself.

3 *✍✍*
THE MEANING OF
SEXUAL INTERCOURSE

We now turn to a theme which all too frequently is lacking or inadequately developed in the typical "home-kit, how-to-do-it" sex manual. We should certainly not minimize the importance of advice, given in books or otherwise, about the physiology and techniques of the sexual act. More important, however, for wholeness of life (and perhaps equally important for successful mechanics) is a sound understanding of the meaning of the act and its purposes.

In a speech in the French Chamber of Deputies on the place of woman in our modern society, in response to a statement that women are different from men, a deputy was reported to have exclaimed, "Vive la différence!" The comment is not as trivial as it may appear. Rightly might we respond to the text in Genesis, "Male and female created He them" with *Laus Deo*— "Thanks be to God." This perennial fact is not the least of God's many blessings to us.

THE EARLIER CHRISTIAN ATTITUDE
TOWARD SEX

If these latter comments seem too obvious, we should recall the history of attitudes towards this subject in our Christian culture. Through the major portion of Christian history the prevailing attitude of the Church was contradictory to such an approach. A dim view of sex—even within marriage, let alone outside of marriage—was characteristic of Christian thought until relatively recent times. Sex was viewed as something best to be avoided, or to be accepted as the lesser of two evils—a necessary concession to human weakness.* Certainly in this country, due to Puritan influence from the beginning and pietistic influence later, sex, indeed joy of any kind, was denigrated. The sexual role of woman was given little place (in contrast to its recognition in a number of primitive civilizations and in classical civilization as reflected in the Greek and Latin poets). It was not particularly expected that a woman would enjoy such relationships; in fact, if she were to indicate that she did, either in words or by marked response, it meant that she was not "nice." In short, her function was to "service" her husband, intercourse being her "duty" and his "right." As a result of this background, until recent times many parents and counselors accompanied their strictures against

* See my *A Time For Christian Candor*, pp. 48–50; for a more complete treatment see D. S. Bailey, *Sexual Relation in Christian Thought* (New York: Harper & Row, 1959).

youthful sexual activity with the picturing of sexual intercourse as dirty, nasty, unclean and "physical" (in contrast to "spiritual"). It is true, people did it when married (as the very presence of the counselee readily attested) ; but marriage created a sort of exception to the rule, as though the parties had taken out a special license to do what basically is a bad thing in itself. Whatever effects such teaching may have had in achieving continence among the unmarried young, it is quite clear that it has had a destructive effect on their potentiality for sexual fulfillment and compatability in marriage itself. For young people who have had it deeply impressed upon them that a certain act is basically unworthy and "not nice," the procuring of a license and the saying of a few words over them by a clergyman will not suddenly change their conscious and unconscious attitudes to positive endorsement. What goes on in marriage is still the same act which for so long had been viewed as bad.

Apart from these unfortunate results of sex instruction grounded on a misvaluation of the sex act itself, it is not clear that this approach has been entirely effective in regard to the diminution of premarital or extramarital sexual activity. For some the denomination of the act as evil simply adds to its fascination. Once illicit relations are tried (and found to be pleasurable) the fact of built-in guilt (along with the secrecy which is the context) can add to the sheer sensuality and enhance the enjoyment. This can lead to a distorted over-rating of the place of sex in life—like the greater danger of incipient alcoholism in persons who have had to sneak drinks from the beginning rather than grow up with them as a taken-for-granted option in refreshments.

A SOUNDER VIEW

In recent decades, happily, Churches have been taking a more constructive line about sex. First of all, it is out in the open. Once it was an unmentionable subject as far as the pulpit went. It was taboo in Christian writings or instruction, not discussed openly and positively in Sunday school classes. Second, there has developed a concept of sexuality more consistent with the basic Judeo-Christian doctrine of Creation. Thus this later position on sex is both new and not new. It is the view I would set forth as the sound fundamental premise for any analysis on the subject with young people.

Two significant sets of words have their place in virtually all religious and ethical systems:

| spiritual | soul | good |
| material | body | bad |

Each of these distinctions has some value in itself; but the tendency in all religious traditions has been to place equal signs between the words in the top line and between the words in the bottom line. To identify the spiritual and the soul with the good and to identify the material and the body with the bad is, speaking broadly, fairly consistent with the theology of some Oriental religions; but it is not at all consistent with the view of reality which is the Biblical doctrine of Creation. A key text is Genesis 1:31: "And on the sixth day the Lord looked down on all that he had made and he said, It is very good." The material, physical and sensual world is not bad; it is good in itself. Both the spiritual and the material are capable of misuse and misdirection and can produce good *or* evil, due to the freedom of men to choose good or evil purposes. The end and purpose of life is not to become more spiritual and less material; man's vocation is to function as one united being, more and more fulfilling his spiritual-material calling under God, with both spirit and flesh moving in the same direction. The flesh and spirit of man are united psychosomatically. From advances in medicine we have learned that there is a mutual inter-action between the spirit and the body in terms of the health of both. But they are not only united psycho-somatically; they are united sacramentally.

SEX AS SACRAMENTAL

A sacrament is "an outward and visible sign of inward and spiritual grace." Sacraments are not only symbols, i.e., means of expressing spiritual reality in relationship; they are also "means of grace" whereby spiritual relationships are fueled. More specifically, in one of the most characteristic human activities in man, namely, in sexual intimacy, not only is there to be seen the means of childbearing; equally important is the fact that there is a sacramental relationship. The physical act not only expresses the spiritual and emotional involvement of a man and woman; it is also a means whereby that involvement is strengthened and "fired up." It is a *good* thing. Any restrictions on it which might be found sound, either from an absolutist or an existentialist approach, should be based on the premise that it *is* a good thing—so good a thing that it should not be utilized under certain circumstances. If your young person's stance toward premarital sex is Maybe, then his decision making in particular cases will be better grounded if his thinking begins with a recognition of the sacramental character of sexual intimacy. And if a young person understands this fundamental premise and decides not to have any sexual relations before marriage, nevertheless he or she will enter marriage with a wholesome and positive view toward the relationship which will then ensue. He or she will feel free fully to enter into it, thanking God for it and glorying in His joy in human fulfillment.

So, if your sons and daughters are to say No, either in general or in particular instances, the *reason* for their No is just as important—or perhaps more important—than the *fact* of the No. If their restraint is based on the fact that sexual intercourse is so good a thing, rather than on the notion that it is so bad a thing, they will enter marriage with a much more wholesome attitude, with much greater likelihood of sound sexual fulfillment in marriage. We will find, too, that a sound understanding of the nature of sex is an important element in understanding the ethics of family planning, later to be discussed.

4 ∽∽

WHEN AND HOW
TO TALK

This book has been constructed on the premise—a sound one—that sex instruction should encompass almost the whole of a child's formative years, from about age five through the late teens. Some of our readers may not have been aware of this fact and have "gotten into the act," as it were, during what is literally "teen-age." This does not mean that all is lost. It is suggested that such a reader nevertheless read the whole book, including chapters that are focused toward instruction of younger children, to be sure that what the parent begins to communicate now also encompasses material which could well have been communicated earlier. It may be that their teen-agers are already caught up with these data and ideas through other sources. But it also may be that their knowledge is somewhat sketchy or that there are serious misconceptions and distortions. Thus in the "catch up" process there must be considerable tailoring of the material to the needs of the given teen-ager and ready discernment of where he is at the time of talking.

OCCASIONS OF COMMUNICATION

Almost as important as the subject matter itself is the *way* parents communicate. This depends upon something more fundamental: the quality and scope of the parent-child relationship in general. One of the most important aspects of a good relationship is the maintenance and development of an open channel (a good analogy is closed circuit TV) between parent and child. If this is descriptive of the actual state of affairs, then, assuming the parent has thought out what he wishes to communicate and the way he seeks both to influence and to understand, there will be no problem about opportunities for instruction and dialogue. The best method of sex instruction is not just a series of formal talks at selected age levels; rather it is communication in a natural way as questions arise and interest manifests itself. Then what is said becomes a significant but emphasized part of ongoing conversation and influence, or to put it more basically, of the *presence* with one another in wholesome family life.

It is ideal when young people—and parents, too, for that matter—can talk naturally about sex in an open manner as part of the general spectrum of interests, news and information. A sign that this atmosphere has been created is when the child or youth first openly shares at home a slightly risqué story. Some advice about this: Do not reflect shock but join in the humor of it. If in the telling, there is indication of misinformation about facts or the projection of a wrong value-pattern, the story can serve as a good springboard for instructional response. Even if it is "dirty," don't freeze up or show disgust, but simply explain why such a story doesn't "go over" very well. Perhaps it would be well to illustrate the distinction by some funny story of your own that has some sexual reference but which is not a dirty story. When there is natural mention of sex in conversation, preoccupation with the matter should be avoided.

In addition to this healthy, casual approach, there are still occasions for taking up the matter of sex in a more organized way. It is important that your children grasp all the factors appropriate to communicate at a given age level, so that they may get a well-rounded picture. This is difficult in any case, and it is often best achieved in an extended session that has been carefully thought through in advance by the instructor and in a place where there is a relaxed atmosphere which will encourage questions and reactions.

It is much better if such sessions do not have to be scheduled, but the chances for unscheduled opportunities for unbroken time presupposes something more basic in the family pattern. Some parents have gotten themselves involved in such a social whirl and/or involvement in community activities that almost all their time with their children is "by appointment" as it were. This denies to the children—and to the parent—the values of spontaneous relationships and sharing, delimiting natural dialogue in the area with which we

41

are concerned as in other areas. It is important for the development of an open atmosphere that parents are often just "around."

In any case, it is important that in the *mind* of the parent there be a pattern of various levels or phases of handling the appropriate material so that over the years natural opportunities can best be taken advantage of when they arise. It is important that by the time certain ages have been reached, given aspects of the subject have been covered, whatever form the coverage has taken. If there is not an adequate open channel, or an adequate free flow of conversational opportunity, then at certain points a staged conversation is called for. While this last outcome is really "the last resort," when it is the case the form of such talks may not be markedly different from extended periods of instruction undertaken at propitious times by parents who are fortunately in a more open relationship with their children. In other words, in even a more natural unstructured pattern of relationship, this subject is too important simply to be covered in "bits and dabs." An analogy: A child does naturally become increasingly interested in the nature of automobiles and in the ways and means of driving one. Obviously the parent will answer particular questions or demonstrate one or another of the aspects of driving all along. Yet a point comes when deliberate driver instruction is undertaken on a systematic basis. The same is true of the learning of arithmetic or a foreign language, no mat-

42

ter how much such subjects have been casually or frag-
mentarily covered in conversations over the early
years.

ATTENTION TO TIMING

The next three chapters deal with three "phases" of
sex instruction. To underline the basic point made
above, this is not meant to imply that a parent's pattern will be simply the provision of three scheduled
lectures. These chapters are provided as a basis for the
latter in families where, for one reason or another,
there is not generally continuous relationship of inquiry and communication in this or in other areas;
and where there is such relationship (and this is de-
voutly to be hoped for) so that the parent may well in
advance have clearly in mind the objectives hopefully
to be achieved through a mixture of casual conversation and, on propitious occasions, of more extended
treatments of the subject.

Whichever approach is the one that eventuates, it is
important that coverage at each level come neither too
early or too late.

Too early: Nothing is more irrelevant than the answer to a question someone has not asked. If a child or
youth has not yet reached the stage of curiosity and
interest about what would be the subject matter of the
given conversation he will either be bored and not
"take it in," or he will be brought to an undue pre-

occupation of one facet of life ahead of what would be a natural development.

Too late: It is important that what you have to say get in the mix during the formative period of children's decision-making in this realm. What you have to say will not necessarily be determinative as to decisions, yet your children should have the right facts. Also, quite reasonably, you hope that your observations will play some part in their weighing of values.

It would be very convenient were one able to specify the precise ages at which particular stages should be reached. But one can't, even by approximation. There are too many variables in regard to each child, his development and his environment. What is most important is the degree of maturity in the child himself. This bears on his capacity to understand and absorb what you will be saying. Quite apart from his overall maturity is the matter of when his natural curiosity and interest in such matters begins to manifest itself. Then, of course, there is the question of when he is apt to begin hearing about these things from others. This is a guess on your part in any event, a guess to be made in the light of the associations he has, the kind of peer group he is involved in and what kind of a community you live in.

SCHOOL INSTRUCTION SUFFICIENT?

Some schools provide sex instruction at what may be regarded by the authorities as appropriate times in the child's development. This can be a very good thing (in spite of the hullabaloo it often causes among certain types of parents in certain communities) ; but it does not discharge *your* responsibility, for a number of reasons :

1. In regard to your particular child in his situation it may come too early or too late.

2. Instruction is generally limited to the physical and social aspects of the matter not extending to the inner meaning and inter-relational aspects in any depth, and not correlated with overall patterns of meaning. This is because of the reticence of public school officials about presenting the religious dimension of any branch of the curriculum, and because of the lack of preparation of the instructor (and this could be true in private schools as well as in public) adequately to present the religio-ethical factors.

3. It is important that one or both parents be in this candid relationship with each of their children, both for the sake of the parent-child relationship itself and for the creation of an atmosphere of openness as a foundation for dialogue in the future.

This last point cannot be stressed too much. Particularly when there has been no discussion of sex between parents and children, but even sometimes when there has been, young people have questions and worries which they somehow feel they have to keep to themselves (or talk about only with others outside the family). They are often shy about raising such matters with their parents; or perhaps they are afraid of parental disapproval, either because of the very fact that they are thinking about the matter or because of a particular turn of events. This possibility may cover the whole span from a child's puzzlement over his first feelings of sexual desire to a young girl's pregnancy. The sooner either of these or anything in between can be aired in an atmosphere of counted-on understanding, the better. At stake is the young person's peace of mind, self-understanding, direction of thought and action, and—in the case of circumstances which are threatening—a wise and prompt solution. It is quite a reflection on the relationship between youth and parent when a young girl carries the burden (in two senses of the word) of pregnancy for months, seeking to "keep the secret" to herself. The same is true, in a measure, when either a son or daughter is worrying about the possibility of a pregnancy or of infection and is afraid to share the worry. More later, on the best way to react to such news as this; but it is important to stress now that the likelihood of your being taken into the confidence of your sons and daughters, should such things eventuate, depends strongly on the foundation which has been laid from the first conversation about sex (as well, of course, as on the general health of the parent-child relationship in all regards).

Church Instruction Sufficient?

Just as in the case of schools, some Churches provide sex instruction for young people at times and in ways which the pastor or the director of educational activities may deem appropriate. Here, of course, there is more likelihood (though it is not necessarily guaranteed!) that the religio-ethical dimension will receive full treatment along with the physical and social aspects. But again, as in the case of the school, the Church cannot serve as a surrogate for you in this regard. Applicable are the two reasons mentioned above, the importance of the right timing (which you as a parent can better sense than the Church in approaching the decision about timing in terms of the group), and the importance of the personal relationship between you and your child—not only for the present, but in terms of the future.

When?

Now we turn to the timing of each of the three phases we will be discussing.

The first phase This should have been completed at a fairly early age, usually when a child is somewhere between five and seven. The timing here is easier to calculate than that of the other two stages. In general we can say that the process should begin when the child first asks questions about his own organs, about those of the opposite sex, about where he came from, and/or about the birth of a newborn baby or of an animal offspring. Made aware of the incipient interest and curiosity, you have your cue.

The second phase   Usually this should come somewhere in the ten to twelve year age level. The cue is in the sign of response to the opposite sex (and, for that matter, towards the same sex) which may soon begin to manifest itself in "crushes" and affectionate friendships. In any case it should have been reached before, but not too long before, the likely beginning of menstruation or of nocturnal emissions. For the young person who has not been previously warned, the first instance of either of these phenomena can be quite traumatic. Fear of physical disorder—and, illogically enough, guilt feelings—can accompany either of these experiences. And often—again, illogically enough— young people are hesitant to mention the fact to their parents. If these phenomena are anticipated in the larger context of discussion, there should be no fear or guilt in connection with their appearance. In the case of beginning menstruation, it can be naturally announced and the practicalities dealt with from the start. Apart from these "outward and visible signs," it is important at this formative stage for young people to have the right facts and the right ideas at the appropriate level of their awareness.

The third phase   In other decades this might well have been postponed until the end of high school. But it would appear that in many communities sexual precociousness has moved up at least a couple of years. Hence, in the case of many young people the third, and much more complete, coverage should have been received midway in high school. If the other two phases have gone well and if there is an open channel of relationship, the danger that this conversing may be delayed too long is minimized. If particular problems and questions arise it is likely that a son or daughter will take up the matter directly; if so, this, whenever it occurs, is perhaps the best time to proceed to an extended coverage of the whole subject.

PREPARING YOURSELF

Many parents, understandably, bring much tension and uncertainty to the demand that they face their job in the sex education of their children. In their own childhood and adolescence they were rarely helped or encouraged toward a comfortable and joyous acceptance of sexuality, one of God's greatest gifts. On the contrary, they were made to feel that sex was something to be hushed up, to be embarrassed about, to be hidden, and deep feelings of fear, shame and tension become attached to the whole area of sexuality. In addition, prudery masquerading as modesty, and suppression hiding under the guise of "morality," were among the requisites for inculcating what little sex guidance might have been offered.

In almost all cultural groups, sexuality in any form was equated with sin and "dirtiness." Worst of all, the subject was avoided, and children and youth were left to struggle alone with real or imaginery fears and worries, crippling to the development of healthy attitudes in adulthood.

49

With this background, parts of which we all share, there is little wonder that today parents quail—when faced with the job of doing a complete "about-face," trying to change deeply ingrained feelings of self-consciousness and tension to attitudes of openness and warm responsive feelings—as they approach the business of guiding their children in this area, so vital in young lives.

The first step for us as parents is to accept these old attitudes consciously and fully in ourselves, to recognize that they exist, and most reassuringly of all, to realize that such feelings of uneasiness, embarrassment, and inadequacy are *perfectly understandable*, perfectly "normal" as it were, considering their source. The second step is to not be threatened by advice often given in books or lectures to "be casual," to "treat this as just one more subject." This is not only poor parent education, it is dishonest, since it suggests a denial of very real feelings deeply implanted in a parent's background. It puts upon the parent the added burden of pretending to be what some books call "gay and easy about the whole thing" when this is an impossible feat for some parents to accomplish.

Be yourself Far sounder is the suggestion that we share honestly our feelings with our youngsters (the youngsters know our real feelings anyway!). In such words as, "You see, Tommy, when Dad and I were young these things were not discussed, people thought it better to avoid the subject. So I'm not exactly expert at it. But I'll help all I can." There is release for the adult who can then proceed, with honesty and with-

50

out trying to be something he or she is not, to meet a child's needs within the bounds of what is realistic for the adult.

Young children's questions are not too difficult to answer. Even the youngest child is aware of underlying uneasiness but he nevertheless accepts factual information quite easily. The school-age child poses a little more difficult demand, since he is a fact seeker and an intelligent questioner (if we have freed him to ask). He will want to have some quite definite information "on the father's part" and other aspects of physical and technical proceedings often difficult for parents to handle on the spot. He accepts with great good nature a phrase such as was quoted above or others like, "I'll need time on that one, Tom; okay if I think about it a little?"—assuming you really need the time, when he has given you a real poser!—These school years, however, are the golden years for guidance such as this book suggests, for two reasons. First, the school-age youngster can accept pretty full information on many aspects of sexuality with considerable openness, lack of tension, and healthy curiosity; and second, the curtain has not yet come down, as it does later when our adolescent may begin to resist not only authority, but sex discussion or instruction as well, with a natural, healthy withdrawal from certain kinds of intimacy with parents. It is important to remember that a parent is not a failure because this withdrawal occurs and because a teen-age youngster pulls back from open discussion of intimate matters. This is, developmentally, part of his way of establishing his own emerging

Self as the adult he will soon become. He will, however, deeply appreciate an openness on the part of his parents toward the whole subject of sex, a willingness to discuss sympathetically, for instance, an incident in a high school group, a current "scandal," or a worry that he may have. We need not fear that showing sympathy and understanding in the sexual and emotional lives of our children will be mistaken for condoning, or for an attitude of anything goes. The important thing is that we recognize that the high school boy or girl terribly needs to know that Mother and Dad's attitudes to him, his world and its dangers and joys, are sympathetic and understanding—not harshly critical or contemptuous. (These last two attitudes often conceal worry and concern on the part of a parent, but alas, they emerge as a destructive barrier between parents and the teen-age youngster.)

IT'S YOUR TASK

As parents face together the inexorable obligation for the guidance in sex education which young people so desperately need today, perhaps the most reassuring fact is this: Children and young people do not mind at all if we are not able to be full of medical facts, instant information and easy responses; they do not mind at all that we are somewhat uncertain, a little inadequate or downright embarrassed as we struggle to give them that guidance.

In fact, they benefit by our honesty in admitting

that we were not educated to be good at this whole business of helping youngsters understand their sexuality, but that we are willing to work hard at it together. They (the children and young people) benefit by seeing, because of our honesty with them, some of the roots of our fears and prejudices, some of the bases of our fears for them, and some of the sources of inevitably differing points of view between generation and generation.

Perhaps the only thing our children cannot forgive us is when we permit our own fears or embarrassments to block off the means of guidance and help they so much need. When we do this—when we allow this blocking to take place—we leave our children *alone*, to struggle with worries, anxieties and questions which no child or young person should be asked to carry by himself.

And we ask ourselves a final question: When I am silent who and what speaks to my child? For sex education takes place everyday of our children's lives—in their schools and on the streets; in their clubs and in their common associations; in our silences or avoidances as well as in our communications and openness. The real decision, and the only one left in our hands, is: Who guides my child when I do not? And with all our uncertainties and all our inadequacies as parents, sex education from us—from parents—is sex education at its best.

5 ✍✍

THE FIRST PHASE

What has been said about the timing of this first phase applies to subject matter as well. We begin where the child is. It is remotely possible that a five-year-old, for example, may have curiosity as to what the sexual act itself is about, but this will only be the case if he has inopportunely entered the bedroom or if perchance he has been told about it by a particularly precocious member of his peer group or by some older person (most unwisely, I would think). It can usually be assumed, however, that he knows nothing about it. But by now there are two things he has doubtless noted:

1. He has probably observed the difference in the genitalia of the two sexes; and
2. He has seen a number of babies and he has heard about new lives coming into the world.

Even apart from these experiences, the time will come when he will display the first phases of the incipient philosophical bent in all of us and begin to wonder how he got here. So in virtually all cases the place to begin is with the miracle of birth.

In times past a kind of tranquilizer for this curiosity was provided by a phony tale: Babies are brought by a stork. Such an answer had the advantage of brevity, but no other advantage. There were several things wrong with it:

1. Underlying the giving of such an answer is the unvoiced assumption that the true facts are not "nice" and, more profoundly, that sex and reproduction are somehow connected with evil (no surprising notion, considering the fact that the Christian Church itself thought this for most of the centuries of its life).

2. Sooner or later (probably sooner) the child will find this tale incredible; he will hear something nearer the true explanation from some other source. This will lead to confusion in his mind and may ultimately lead to mistrust of his parents.

This opens a broader problem. In a number of realms parents supply fanciful explanations to their children, assuming that these are more appropriate for the given age level. Adults who for themselves would not be willing to affirm absolutely the existence of angels in any traditional sense think it's fine for their young children to believe in angels. Many parents who are not fundamentalist about the Bible present all Biblical stories to their young people as flat facts. Sometimes this is true, too, of the presentation of Biblical narratives to young people in Sunday Schools of non-fundamentalist Churches. In the case of those illustrations, the children's confrontation in later years with a more sophisticated approach to Biblical literature may be traumatic and may lead to rejection of religious faith altogether. A young person whose religious education has not been dealt with honestly and who has not begun to learn to separate the wheat from the chaff, or fact and plausible belief from poetry and meaningful myth, is a sitting duck for the destruction of his faith. His secularist instructors and others with whom he will later come in contact may easily poke holes in the youth's assumptions about quite nonessential matters. The fact that a particular Biblical narrative is not historically supportable does not in the least militate against religious faith in the Judeo-Christian tradition. If a child has been taught that all these things are equally true and then later sees that certain portions of the tradition do not hold water on a historical basis, he may well "throw the baby out with the bath water."

Therefore nothing (repeat, nothing) should be told a child which the parent (according to his own religious lights) would not expect the child to believe as an adult. Let's take an example which has nothing to do with sex (angels are supposed to be sexless) : In the coverage of angels with my children I at no point confirmed their literal reality, yet at the same time I did not exclude this imagery from the child's religious

56

picture. My approach was something like this, "When we talk about angels and see pictures people have drawn of angels, we really don't know if there are beings like that flying around (we don't know that there are not, either), but the idea of angels does picture for us something about God. He is everywhere, and is as close to each of us as breathing, and has unlimited power in the ways of helping and supporting us. These ways are shown in a great variety (there are supposed to be nine kinds of angels in tradition) and each of us in our needs is *special* to him and his tie to each of us is special."

This is not a diversion from the subject at hand. It is meant as an analogy for our approach to sex instruction. We need not (and should not) at each age level communicate everything we know about the subject (truly applicable here, in regard to consideration of certain subject matters at certain age levels, is the maxim "silence is golden"). But what we do say should be *true*—not to be unlearned later or subject to debunking when we are not around to help pick up the pieces.

What is needed throughout this first phase is *truth, with a light touch.*

A number of helpful booklets for young children, and guides for parents in presenting the facts of reproduction, are available and are listed in the bibliography. Here we seek only to outline the general approach.

One can go directly to human reproduction, or begin with a nondetailed explanation of reproduction among other categories of living beings. If we use the latter approach it is important that our purposes are clear cut: It is not that we want to be oblique or dodge the really important matter, but rather that we want to communicate the universality of the reproductive process in creation so that human reproduction will not appear to be something odd.

In any case, it should be explained that in the case of the birth of a human baby, the infant comes from inside the mother where the egg has already grown and developed, and that the father has taken a part in the matter about nine months before birth and, in general terms, how. It is important to stress immediately that that activity was part of the father's expression of his love for the mother—like expressions which the child has already seen: kissing, hugging and other forms of closeness, in and out of bed. It may be said that it can happen when the father and mother are very close to each other, that they want to be close anyway since they love each other, and that *sometimes* when they are this close a child is started on its way. To state this at this point is fairly important, in order to anticipate and possibly forestall common illusions which can arise later, namely that conception occurs on each occasion of intercourse, or (believe it or not, a misconception of mine when I was about ten) that nine months of nightly intercourse was necessary, without missing a night, for a baby to be produced!

Since a child has probably noticed that his mother and other women become rather heavy in the months

preceding birth, it might be wise at this point to reveal that this usually has meant that a baby is in
there, growing and developing. In fact, it would be
well to tell the child that he or she had his beginning
this way, growing day by day inside his mother. You
can go further and explain that the mother generally
goes to the hospital when the time comes, that when
the baby first comes out there is a little cord connect-
ing the mother and the child which is a means of the
nourishment of the child when he is inside the mother,
and that this cord is not needed anymore once the
child is born—and, too, that is the reason for his navel.
The child may also have observed breast-feeding;
hence this might be a good time to explain the continuation of the relationship of the mother to the physical
development of the child.

Whether more or less than this should be told at this
point is of course up to the discretion of the parent.
But more important than what is actually told or the
words used in its telling (the vocabulary should depend on the factors appropriate to any other conversation with children, in terms of adequate communication), is the spirit in which it is told and the mood of
the teller. Here are some important pointers:

1. The child should be helped to feel that there is
    a great joy about all this—not only in the birth
    of the baby and the expectation through the
    months, but in the expression of love which
    started the process.

2. You should get across the fact that close physi-

59

cal expression of love between parents is a good thing in itself, and that whether a baby will be started on its way generally depends upon a decision to bring another life into the family. Here it is neither necessary nor appropriate to summarize the methods of birth control. It is sufficient that it be made clear to the child that he was *wanted*, and that the mind as well as the body entered into the outcome. This may not be directly significant to the child at this point; but it is another way of assuring the child that he is loved. In any case it lays a good foundation for the presentation, during the second phase, of the two purposes of sexual intercourse.

3. A basic religious dimension should be included from the start and should be expressed in terms appropriate to the child's capacity to grasp it: In and under all things he can see (and many things he can't see) is the Source of all life and part of His plan is to bring into the world all kinds of creatures. And, more specifically, He is the Source of all the things which go into the coming into the world of a new baby. This is a sign of His power and goodness, and our joy in this is part of His joy.

If communication is already good between parent and child, the child may well have some questions. He may take the conversation further than the parent had planned (and further than the foregoing outline). In general, it is better not to answer such questions by cutting them off. Don't say: "You are too young to know about that" or "I'll be telling you about that later on." This will only increase the degree of premature curiosity and develop an atmosphere contradictory to the mood of candor which you wish to establish from the beginning. It is much better to try to answer the question, in generalized terms if it involves data too complex for the child to grasp or facts which at this age might give undue attention to certain matters. Here particularly the parent must "play it by ear": there is no way that a manual like this can provide specifics for answering.

Not as a distraction from further questions, but as a way of tying things up in context and of stressing the fact that his own coming into the world is not some kind of oddity, it might be well to teach him a stanza from a familiar hymn:

> All things bright and beautiful,
> All creatures great and small,
> All things wise and wonderful,
> The Lord God made them all.*

* Found in many hymn books (e.g., The [Episcopal] Hymnal 1940, Hymn 311). Though various aspects of creation are covered, human reproduction is not mentioned specifically: perhaps it is because the hymn was written in 1848! But human birth is certainly embraced within the adjective petition of the "All" in the refrain quoted above, and all children are potentially, if not actually, "wise" and all are "wonderful."

6 ⚬⚬

THE SECOND PHASE

The writing of this chapter is harder for the author and the fulfillment of the task it covers will be harder for the parent. While no two children are alike even in infancy, we are now dealing with an age span where individuality in children develops more and more distinctively by the week. The approach had to be tailored even at the earlier age; and this is more the case in the second phase. Further, no matter what has been decided upon as appropriate to say, if the lines of parent-child communication are good the child's comments and questions are likely to get the parent "in deeper" than he had anticipated. On the other hand, the parent may sense diffidence or disinterest in certain areas which he assumed would, during this period, be relevant to the child. The former contingency suggests that the parent should be much more fully prepared than seems to be called for in the scope he intended to cover, just as the preparation of any teacher should encompass a great deal more than he plans to go through in a given lesson. As to the latter possibility, except in matters which he deems essential for the child to know because of impending developments (e.g., menstruation or nocturnal emission), the parent should be prepared to "skip a band" in the record and move on to where interest is discerned.

HOW TO BEGIN

It can be assumed that by this time (10–12), when the child is approaching his teens, he is interested in human reproduction and wants to know more about it than he has learned before. Also he probably will have become markedly curious about sex itself, either from his awareness of sexual feelings or from reading, television, movies or conversation. It is likely that he has experienced sexual attraction. Whether the child or the parent opens the matter, early in the discussion the child may say something which may unnerve the parent, though it shouldn't. Even with a wholesome home atmosphere and a consistent pattern of candor between parents and children, some self-consciousness is to be expected. It will be rewarding for both if most of the conversation displays a seriousness of attitude, but a parent should not be put off or thrown by signs of self-consciousness. Here one must "roll with the punches," and for this reason, among others, there should be more opportunities providing a substantial stretch of undisturbed time for these talks.

It would be well to "recap" what has been said before, but very briefly. By now, most of that early data is pretty well understood and taken for granted. Don't give the impression that you are going to cover the same ground, like a sort of "review." Reviews are already somewhat distasteful to schoolchildren. Actually the best "opener" would be to assume that the child has a considerable degree of knowledge and by almost casual questions try to discover to what extent that assumption is correct. Then proceed to fill the gaps by moving on without delay to a brief outline of what you are going to talk about: What goes on between the mother and father at conception and what goes on in the mother till the time of birth. It is not the purpose of this book to provide this material, since there are a number of manuals listed in the bibliography at the end of the book, which afford good descriptions.

WHAT TO COVER

A description of the female and male organs should be included; not overly detailed but more complete than during the first phase. For this purpose pictures and sketches in books like those mentioned can be shown to a child; but you should not use this method if you are not prepared to have the child read the whole book that is put into his hands. In any case, it is better that the parent familiarize himself with the pictures sufficiently and be able to sketch out roughly the sex organs and their locations as he talks. This will create a greater spirit of naturalness and confidence in the parent's direct knowledge, and will also help defeat self-consciousness. Helpful, too, are gestures describing the location of the sex organs and parts.

There should be some description of the sexual act itself. At this age, however, it is not appropriate or necessary to go into the matter of various sexual techniques, the achievement of orgasm, fore-play, after-play, etc.

In discussing the purpose of sex, it would be better not to touch on an unspoken assumption, reflected, of course, in the way things are put, that you are talking about sex within marriage. Whether or not the parent's view is conventional or liberal, it is not likely that plans for heterosexual activity have yet developed in the mind of the child. In any case, under either of the two basic approaches the answer would be pretty clearly the same at this age-level. Even under the liberal view, immaturity alone would pretty generally preclude sound weighing in terms of likely effects. Under either an existentialist approach or an absolute approach, the answer is No, anyway. So there is no point in getting into the whole question of the physical aspects of sex unless the child himself raises it.

In turning to sex itself it would be well to start with the recognition that sexual feelings are common to most people at this stage of development, and that this is good, being part of the continuing plan for our lives.

The two purposes of sexual relationship should be explained: procreation of children and the sacramental purpose reflected in love of the couple for each other. Marriage should be described as a social arrangement best designed for fulfillment of these purposes, providing a type of companionship no other relationship does—one which can unify the various aspects of the personalities of each partner. It should be pointed out that this pooling of hopes and fears, strengths and weaknesses, is expressed most fully in the sexual embrace, which in turn serves to nourish and strengthen the overall union.

This has been mentioned before, but should be stressed again—not so much by words (though they may be useful), but by the manner and mood of the instructor: *the genuine joy of the marriage relationship and of sexual expression should be made apparent.*

Even if the right age has been chosen for such conversation, the child may be but dimly able to apprehend the sense of positive enjoyment in intercourse. It should be said outright that though this pleasure cannot be described it is a fact, and that this will doubtless be appreciated in due time.

Here is a summary of what we want to be sure to discuss. We have already analyzed approaches to most of this subject matter.

1. The purpose of marriage and the purposes of sex within marriage.
2. The nature and operation of the sexual organs

involved in intercourse and childbirth (in general outline).

3. The nature of the sexual act itself (in general outline).
4. Menstruation and nocturnal emission.
5. Caution as to certain decisions and dangers relevant to this age and the immediate years ahead.

This latter category has not yet been covered and now will be given separate attention.

APPROPRIATE CAUTIONS

There is a real difficulty here. As parents we do not wish to plant ideas that may prematurely stir curiosity and action (or develop fear of later action). We do not want to present a problem to our children before they are ready for a discussion of the problem. On the other hand, we do not wish them to be subjected—at a time when we will not be present for on-the-spot advice or caution—to fears, influences, or actions which, particularly during this period of their development, are likely to be deleterious to them. In short, although we do not want to frighten or push them we do want to prepare them in time for what may be coming up. A wise balancing of these factors as to the subject matter outlined depends very much (as does wise adaptation of the whole subject matter to a particular child), on the sensitivity, perception and discretion of the parents.

From experience, personal and vicarious, I am

67

afraid that I have to report that a parent will feel quite uncertain as he proceeds in this realm. Of course, if all along there has been the "open channel," the child may reflect the degree of his awareness of these problems and even speak on his own of certain experiences, thoughts, or desires. This will help. So, to the degree that there is curiosity or candor already present, the child's questions will give some guidance. Particularly in these areas, it is generally not safe to say nothing, and it is generally not wise to say too much.

Masturbation   There is conflict of attitude on this subject. On the one side, most medical and psychological authorities regard masturbation as a normal part of a person's sexual development. On the other side, some religious traditions—and therefore, not surprisingly, many parents—regard masturbation as evil. In any case, there are few parents whose views make appropriate the positive encouragement of this activity; at the other end, there are fewer and fewer these days who wish to repeat the monitory and terrifying strictures with which they were perhaps familiar in their own youth. However, wherever parents stand in this whole swing of the pendulum, there are certain clear "don'ts."

1.   As a plain matter of fact (supported by various statistical studies), a very high percentage of young people will practice masturbation, beginning at various age levels (hence the indication in the preceding chapter that in some cases this topic might well be taken

up earlier than "the second phase") and continuing at varying degrees of frequency. It must be recognized that nothing that you say is apt to form a conclusive barrier, even if that is your desire. Therefore, it is important that there not be engendered in the child fears which will be unduly destructive to his self-esteem and to his general psychological and physical health.

In this connection, it is obvious that statements should not be made which are simply not true. For example, in times past it was customary to say that masturbation led to serious debilitation of the body and insanity. While it is true that excessive masturbation has been noted in the cases of some persons afflicted with mental illness, this masturbatory activity is a *symptom*, among others, of imbalance, and not the *cause* thereof. Although it is true that, as in the case of *any* other activity, there is a point of excess that can be physically debilitating, there is, in general, no correlation between masturbation and mental and physical health, apart from the effects of fears engendered by parents or others. Nor are such fears minimal in result. If the child believes firmly that masturbation affects his mind, it possibly will; and because of the psychosomatic nature of the human organism, if a child believes that it will cause loss of physical energy and coordination, it doubtless will. Here is a legend which you can make come true. Don't.

2.   We have already stressed that a negative evaluation should not be attached to sexual intercourse— that it is "nasty" or "unclean." Nor should such be at-

tached to masturbation. If your stated opposition could be guaranteed to prevent its occurring, the use of such words might be advisable. But since it will in most children occur anyway, there is no use to take the considerable risk of creating a self-destructive attitude and one which can easily spread in the child's conscious or unconscious mind to sex in general.

3. On the basis of evidence discovered from examination of underwear, pajamas, or bedsheets, do not make charges in the fashion of a prosecuting attorney. On the other hand, even the most liberal parents on becoming aware of genuine excess or preoccupation with this activity, should feel called upon to consult a physician or psychiatrist and follow his lead as to the approach to be made, either directly, or through him.

So much for the "don't." As for the actual content of what you say on this topic, it will depend upon your basic point of view. If your opinion is in accord with the recognized medical and psychological one there may be no need to say anything, unless you are asked about the subject (or, where appropriate, as indicated above, in the case of signs of genuine excess or preoccupation).

However, if the ethics of your religious tradition or your personal convictions require that you judge such activity as sinful, and if after critically reexamining such presuppositions you still hold the same convictions, then you will want to plant the basis for restraint on the part of your children. If this is the case, remember that prohibition or denomination as a sin may not in itself necessarily produce the desired result. It would be better to say—and this would be a good thing for a parent holding any view to say, because it is true—that sexual desires are primarily implanted that we might have fulfillment with other persons, and that therefore solitary sexual gratification is neither as physically fulfilling nor as spiritually fulfilling as the use of sex in the way in which it was primariy intended to be used. You may also point out the danger that the solitary satisfaction, which is very *ersatz*, can with some persons come to stand in the way of the greater thing which is to come. It also can be pointed out—and this is also the truth—that there is no need for "relief" on a basis of physical health, for nature has provided other ways, e.g., the nocturnal emission. The parent can frankly recognize that there will be sexual desires and arousals (or already have been) ; but he can stress that such can serve as an image of what will come in later years, and that one's mind can be focused on the greater fulfillment. Thus what is present at this time can enhance what is to come, rather than possibly militate against it through a pattern of partial fulfillment now.

There is no guarantee that making these points will result in self-restraint on the part of your children. But they are as likely—or more likely—to achieve this as will a flat prohibition (with pronouncement of sanctions) and the pinning of negative labels on the activity.

Homosexual expression   There is also a division of

71

opinion, though on this by far the greater majority would favor the conventional view, on how homosexual activity is to be judged. There are many who endorse the almost (but not quite) universal criminal sanctions for such conduct, and while there are a growing number who wish the repeal of laws prohibiting homosexual conduct between free-consenting adults, most of these same persons regard the conduct itself as evil or undesirable.

On the other hand (and this number is growing too, which does not mean that the idea is therefore sound), others would remove this conduct—at least on the part of free-consenting persons—from the category of "sin." There are some who do not even regard it as a deviation, but simply as an alternate plan of life and sexual expression. But very few indeed (including those in the latter category) are favorable toward inculcation of homosexual tendencies in young people.

Modern depth psychology has made us aware that there is a homosexual component in almost everyone, most individuals differing in this regard only in the percentage of masculine-feminine makeup. It is also understood that aspects of our sexuality can be increased or decreased by the influence of others and by environment. To whatever degree a parent would be able (or is prepared in advance) to accept a predominantly homosexual son or daughter in his adult years, few would wish homosexual activity to be encouraged during the formative years. Yet the fact is that there is considerable chance that such encouragement may occur without the direct knowledge of the parent.

It is hoped that the candor during the first and second phases will have reduced the child's unfulfilled curiosity about sex organs. But, to the degree this curiosity still exists, it is quite commonplace for young people of more or less the same age level to examine each other's organs, touch them, and from that go on to and seek to engage in other contacts, possibly mutual masturbation. In itself, this activity does not necessarily reflect a sexual imbalance or determine future preferences. But the fulfillment may seem to be satisfying (especially if the emphasis on a much more complete satisfaction has not been communicated by the parent or others). If this practice continues long enough it can indeed focus the reality of sexual fulfillment on persons of the same sex, and can have a definite bearing on development in the homosexual direction.

Specific knowledge of such instances on the part of the parents should not cause undue alarm, nor should elements of fear and fright be inculcated in the child. Nevertheless, there is a sufficient possibility of deflection here (and it is not a remote one) to make it appropriate for a parent to give a brief, generalized introduction to the subject of homosexuality along the lines of the comments above. Thus it can be hoped that a child can himself see the reasons that it is better not to make a pattern of engaging in sexual activities with persons of the same sex.

Some older homosexuals (but apparently a minority of them) have a preoccupation with relationships with children and youths. Here there is danger of actual

73

seduction. The seducer has a number of cards he can play: an already developed admiration for, and liking of the older person, trusting him in whatever he might do or propose; petty bribes or threats; and/or rewarding sexual stimulus, pleasing to the child. It is regrettable, but a fact, that some adults and older youths charged with educational responsibility for younger persons take advantage of the relationship. Yet it is obviously undesirable, indeed impossible, for a parent totally to withdraw his child from all such adult contacts. The same is true in terms of most twosome activities. No parent would want to adopt a flat rule that his child never goes anywhere with an adult of the same sex; at the same time some alertness on the part of the parent is important, and whispered conversations or overeagerness of an adult in repeated invitations, "knowing looks" between the adult and the child should be amber lights. Coupled with a certain degree of parental watchfulness should be inculcation of the practice of caution on the part of the child himself.

We should remember that young people (adults, too, for that matter) have an inherent block against tattling or "finking" (the more current term). The idea should be made clear that this kind of influence is basically "a bad thing," both regarding your own child and others; therefore you should indeed be informed of any "passes" or pressures toward this end. Be prepared in advance for the possibility that they may not comply with this reasonable request, but if the whole matter is presented rightly, one can hope that one's children will, on their own, reject such approaches and drop the company of those who make them.

Heterosexual activity In our time there is more precociousness in this matter than most parents realize. At fairly young ages there is often mutual inspection and manual contact, parallel to the same between persons of the same sex. And there may not have developed any sense of wrong or guilt about this; just plain "play" may be the only conscious attitude. Even before sexual entry has been contemplated or proposed, not uncommon is manual, or even oral contact of organs. More common is kissing, which can be sufficiently sustained to result in sexual arousal. Therefore, it should not be surprising that when opportunity affords, actual entry is not infrequently attempted or achieved. The likelihood can be greater when one of the partners is somewhat older and perhaps has already had experience with persons of his own age group. Of course, some older youths or adults attempt—or succeed—in what for them is statutory rape.

There are differing attitudes on the part of parents as to intercourse, in various circumstances, between unmarried persons. However, virtually no parents would feel that this activity is good on the part of children of the ages we are talking about. If for no other reason, there is the fact of immaturity, disqualifying young teen-agers from making discriminating judgments as to either the engagement in the activity itself or the persons with whom it is engaged in.

But even here it is unlikely that the parental No or the ecclesiastical No will in itself guarantee compliance. To be communicated are the reasons for the child himself to say No. These reasons have been sufficiently covered already. But in addition, words of caution should be sounded. It is possible that others, in their own peer group or older, may seek to seduce them and the comments already made in connection with possible homosexual approaches, are applicable here.

Although in this chapter a great amount of space has been given to outlining these cautionary items they should not occupy this proportion of time in the conversations themselves. Here, as in many other important realms of life, is applicable the cliché: "Accentuating the positive."

Parents should always keep in mind that a balance must be met between communication of a positive joyful attitude towards sex and prudent appraisal of the hazards ahead. The best intentioned instruction on the part of parents has sometimes given the child (especially where the degree of sexual desire is nonexistent or at a low ebb) an attitude something like this: "From what I hear, as far as I'm concerned I don't want ever to have anything to do with it at all." Very few parents (unless they have high hopes that their son or daughter will adopt the monastic life) would regard this as the optimum outcome of their efforts at sexual instruction of their children.

7 ♊

THE THIRD PHASE

E ven more than in the case of the previous two phases, the planning and the initial approach in the third phase will depend very much on where the youth is, as indicated by questions he has asked and comments he has made, as well as upon what you have been able to discern about the attitudes and activities of his peer group. And even more, by this time, your son and daughter will have picked up a great deal from other sources—some of it sound and some of it unsound, some of it factual and some of it legend. Therefore, it is a little more difficult to be able to provide a precise pattern for the parent.

Care should be taken to make clear that you are talking on a more mature level, so that a "ho-hum" response will not begin to deaden the atmosphere of conversations on this subject. When in doubt, take the risk of being too "adult," rather than of being too "juvenile," in what you say and even in the words you use. If you err on the adult side, a question and answer can clarify; if you err on the juvenile side, boredom (and even resentment) may result.

As in the case of the second phase, it would be generally wise to begin with emphasis on marriage and of sexual intercourse within it. This material has already been covered (see Chapter 3). Even parents taking the liberal point of view really won't turn on a green light; at most, it will be an amber rather than a red light. Here, the approach on the part of a liberal parent and that of a parent following conventional views, will merge. As we have pointed out in several connections, a flat No or prohibition, even on the part of the latter category of parents, is not too likely to achieve, unaided, the results intended. Hence the factors outlined, which for such parents will be the *reasons* for a No result, are the *factors* which a liberal parent will want to have the son or daughter weigh in the decision-making about whether to go ahead or not. The more conventional parent would hope, for example, that the communication of the sacramental nature of sex would be sufficient to cause the youth to say No to any premarital sexual activity; liberal parents would hope that the inculcation of this attitude would result in a No in many instances of contemplated activity. What has been said in previous chapters, along with other factors which the parents may deem significant, applies to both categories of parents.

On the other hand, neither should use for a "No" (or even a "maybe not") answer arguments which no longer hold water or unduly stress those which do not carry too much weight either with the parents or in the minds of young people (see pp. 17–21).

Whatever the parents' basic ethical system, whatever their judgment is as to how things should be "tailored," especially in talking to youths in this particular stage of development and experience, it is of crucial importance (and I stress it again at the risk of being repetitious) that the approach be "sexual intimacy is so good a thing that . . ." and not "sexual intimacy is so bad a thing that. . . ."

KISSING, NECKING, PETTING

The analysis in this book, has largely revolved around the Yes/No as to sexual intercourse. But actually for most young people there is an in-between question (for some perhaps the only conscious question), namely, the rightness of various degrees of intimacy short of full sexual communion. Different phrases have been used in different decades and subcultures to differentiate between various degrees of activity: necking, petting, heavy petting. (There is a modern more generalized phrase: making out.) Included in the range is everything from holding hands or a brief goodnight kiss, to petting and mutual masturbation to orgasm. Within this range nothing is left out except actual sexual entry, thus retaining "technical virginity."

There are few parents who would pronounce a flat prohibition on all physical contacts within the range;

for example, seldom heard these days is the dictum that couples should not kiss until their engagement. (One young lady so instructed asked me in bewilderment, "Then how does a girl get engaged?") Even under a *Code* ethic no one has been able to state with very much accuracy "where to draw the line." Any approach to the question from an absolute point of view would involve two facets: (1) that certain contacts between unmarried persons are sinful in themselves; and (2) that, apart from this, "one thing leads to another." Thus certain things which might otherwise not be viewed as sins in themselves are viewed as "occasions of sin." Under such an approach the line would seem to be drawn just short of sexual arousal. But the interlocking of the conscious mind, unconscious mind and the body are such that it is difficult for individuals to discern where the line actually *is* between non-arousal and arousal. Actually there are factors of arousal in just "being together" when there is immediate attraction and sharing of ideas and experience; in a different atmosphere where there is less communication and less attraction, an actual contact "further down the line" could be relatively nonarousing.

Analyzing the same matter from an *existential* point of view does not provide any definite answers either. "Guide lines" can be suggested:

1. In the context of the particular tie is the given form of expression appropriate to the degree of relationship existing between the two persons? Within the single broad word "love," there is

quite a variety in the degrees of depth and breadth.*

2. Since sex, being sacramental, *fuels* relationship, it should be asked, "How deep do we want this love to become?"

3. If these considerations provide limits, then can we do x without compulsively moving to y or z?

Some of the gradational words now in use are rapport/recognition/commitment. A somewhat more familiar set of categories is like/love/in love. Actually for the many possible levels of relationhip there are simply not enough words and the few we have are very imprecise.

Since we are physical-spiritual beings, at every level of relationship some form of physical contact is common from a handshake on out. It is obvious that we cannot provide a detailed chart precisely correlating what forms of physical expression are appropriate to what degree of relationship. Even if, theoretically, it would be possible to devise such a chart it could at best only spell out what might be appropriate for two individuals whose relationship is not dynamic or "moving," in exact "parity" and with no other relationships on the part of either. But since boy-girl associations rarely meet these conditions, such "charting" is impossible. But the guide lines listed above can be pointed out, as well as the considerations treated in the chapter on "Emotional Involvement."

* See more fully my *Doing the Truth*, ch. 13.

However, as to the full act the discussion should not be "over" with the statement of a prohibition and the reasons supporting the No answer (or of factors to be weighed before deciding to go ahead, in the case of some parents) . This would be ostrichlike indeed. Since the fact is that a considerable portion of youths are going to go ahead, no matter what parents or the Church say, instruction should proceed with open recognition of this contingency.

BUT IF ...

We now take up the most controversial question in regard to the approach to sex education these days. The parent who believes that premarital sex is, under certain circumstances at least, acceptable, will have no difficulty at this point. But the parent who is firmly against such activity, in any and all circumstances, will be in real doubt as to whether anything at all should be said to young people on the assumption that they may go ahead. The doubt relates to the necessary weighing of two factors:

1. To talk to our young people about responsibilities within premarital sexual activity could be interpreted as encouraging such activity or implying it is all right; or, at the least, it could display an attitude of giving up hope that they will practice continence.

2. Since, regardless of what we say, a high per-

centage of unmarried young people do in fact engage in premarital sex, there is naturally a desire to reduce to a minimum possible harmful consequences.

This weighing each parent must do for himself; there is no absolute answer. What follows is written for those who in pondering these factors have come to the conclusion that all things considered, it is better to speak further about the matter in the light of the possibility (not a fatuous one, when you know the statistics) that the young person may in fact engage in sexual intercourse or a high degree of sexual intimacy before marriage.

Should such advice be deliberately undertaken, it would seem to involve four areas: (1) birth control, (2) venereal disease, (3) discretion, and (4) decent treatment of one's sexual companions. All of these (and perhaps others) are components of the ethics of responsibility within a relationship, or set of relationships, which in themselves may or may not be approved of. Such a category of ethics we are familiar with in other connections. Even a person who does not approve of divorce under any circumstances would grant that a divorced person has ethical responsibility to his former spouse and to his children. And it is not extreme to suggest that a professional thief (however unethical his basic conduct may be) has certain ethical responsibilities within his professional life, e.g., not needlessly to injure or kill his victims. Even those who take a dim view of gambling generally expect gamblers to pay their gambling debts and not to use marked cards.

BIRTH CONTROL

Not long ago the mother of a senior at a nearby college came to me for counsel when she learned of her daughter's pregnancy. Her sense of distress and shame centered around the fact that her daughter had committed fornication. But when at the mother's request I saw the daughter (principally to talk about whether or not the couple should be married), wrongly or rightly I immediately zeroed in on this question, "How could the two of you—seniors in college—have been so irresponsible as not to have taken precautions?" Quite apart from the morality of the behavior which caused conception, this seemed to be the immediate existential ethical question, and the one which would throw some light on the maturity of the parties—one aspect of the evaluation of their readiness for marriage.

This is a sound ethical principle: A moral decision having been made (wrongly or rightly), ethical responsibility continues within the context created by the prior decision. Therefore, in this particular field it does seem sound to say that *if* the couple is going to go ahead before marriage, they have a serious responsibility to practice birth control. How far a given parent may wish to go in instruction in this regard, or how far a parent may wish to cooperate in the implementa-

tion of the advice, is a matter for each to decide.
(Needless to say, even without parental instruction
most young people in their older teens know of one or
two methods of birth control which are rather easy for
them to practice.) In any case, two other points should
be covered in this regard:

1. The teen-ager should be encouraged to inform
   one or both parents at the first sign of pregnancy, so that the young person need not carry
   the burden alone and may have some mature
   guidance. This thought should be communicated in a way that will make clear that there
   need be no fear of such an announcement as
   far as the familial relationship is concerned.

2. There should be some coverage of the matter of
   marriage in relationship to pregnancy. There
   was a day when the sense of family disgrace
   over unmarried pregnancy was so great, and
   the ways and means of coping with the situation
   in the community so minimal, that the only
   answer seemed to be a marriage under duress.
   Particularly relevant then was the story about
   the young couple who approached the clerk for
   a marriage license. On looking them over, the
   clerk said to the boy, "You look old enough,
   but I'm afraid your fiancée will have to have
   her father's consent." "Who do you think that
   is at the door," the boy retorted, "Daniel
   Boone?"

Fortunately, times have changed. There is more general recognition of the fact that one misfortune should not be compounded by another. This implies a greater respect for marriage; there should be a more substantial basis for marriage than simply the fact that a child is expected. In fact, to enter matrimony for that reason alone is sacrilegious. Assuming that the putative birth is the result of a definite known relationship, then the question should be raised—and this is the same question which would be raised if a child were not expected—does this couple have the "makings" of a sound marriage.

If the partners love each other and were planning to marry in due time anyway, and if on sober reflection a sound marriage could be anticipated, the answer could well be Yes; and the fact of pregnancy will have an important bearing on the setting of the date for the nuptials. But if the parties are not in love—and, even when they are if they otherwise would not have married, and should not marry—then the answer should be No. If the marriage has poor chances, then a "shot gun wedding" is the borrowing of further grief. And in no case should there be a marriage with the intent to procure an annulment and divorce immediately thereafter; this is sheer fraud, both on the Church and on the State. The modern legal situation no longer makes it important to take this particular step just "to give the child a name." There are no legal disabilities for "bastardy" anymore (and, in fact, the Roman

Catholic Church has recently removed this as an impediment to ordination).

Further, the social milieu has changed in most strata of modern life. It would now be an exaggeration to say that a girl is "ruined" because of an "illegitimate" pregnancy. There are circumstances—psychological and physical—which in some states make legal abortion possible (this is all the more reason for the point made above, that young persons should be urged to notify their parents immediately should such an unfortunate outcome occur).

Even if the marriage would otherwise have had a fair chance of success, to marry just because of the pregnancy is to build into the situation conscious and unconscious resentments, which of themselves can be quite destructive to the chances of a happy marriage. A first marriage followed by divorce or annulment will require later explaining, whereas if the pregnancy is handled with discretion no explaining may be necessary in the years to come. If marriage does not occur, and the birth proceeds, with arrangements made for adoption, as complicated and heartrending as all this may be there is at least the knowledge that a benefit has been conferred upon some childless couple. In some circumstances, the mother may keep the baby; there have been many instances when this has been a happy outcome, when "digested" with understanding in the context of a future marriage—one which does have a sound basis.

87

Some parents may feel that the subject should not be gone into at this point, but only at the time when this particular situation may arise. However, there is a connection between points 1 and 2. If point 2 *is* covered, it will increase the likelihood that the young person will carry through with point 1, namely, feel free to open up as to the facts should a pregnancy occur.

There is another analogy to support the position of those parents who have deemed it best to carry the discussion this far: A new driver is informed that should he recklessly damage a parked vehicle he should stop and leave the appropriate information in a secure place on the other vehicle, and he should report the accident to the authorities. Few people would regard the passing out of these instructions as an invitation to reckless driving. Rather, taking into account the possibility of reckless driving, the instruction is the declaration of an ethical responsibility which has been embodied in statutory law (and which, incidentally, would be ethically required even if there were no statutes on the subject).

Venereal Disease

We all know there has been a great deal of medical progress in the cure of syphilis, gonorrhea, and other venereal diseases. Yet at the same time statistics show an increase in the incidence of such diseases, and it would seem that no class of society is exempt from the reflection of this increase. Therefore it is not a dead subject much as we wish it were.

Some parents might feel that this subject is irrelevant—if their young people did proceed they would not be promiscuous and would not have relations with promiscuous persons. This is suitable enough as a hope. Nevertheless, the pattern cannot be guaranteed. Nor is there complete candor among young people (any more than there is among adults) as to what relationships with other companions they may have currently or have had in the past. Further, a person may not be aware that he is infected: it is possible for persons of either sex to be carriers of disease without experiencing evident symptoms themselves.

How far a parent will wish to go in instruction as to immediate precautions after intercourse is a matter for each parent to weigh on the basis of considerations already summarized. In any case it hardly seems improper to alert young people to the symptoms and urge them to "report in" should any of these symptoms show themselves, so that immediate medical help may be arranged. Here, of course, it is obvious that it is not only for their own benefit (and care of one's health is an ethical responsibility) but for the safety of others in our common society—also an ethical responsibility.

Discretion

Since our culture is in the confluence of two views about extramarital sex, then regardless of the soundness of either view the plain fact is that those who hold and/or act out the liberal view can incur criticism (and perhaps even sanctions affecting the future) from those holding the more conservative view. Concern for this matter is not merely one of self-regard, in the nonethical sense. Self-regard, insofar as factors are concerned bearing on one's future possibilities of vocational and marital fulfillment in life, is in itself part of ethical obligation. But also there is an obligation to the partner and to parents, for whom it may well be important that there be an air of respectability in "the family's reputation."

It is easy, for young people especially, to say "I don't care what other people think"; in fact, it can be a good attitude when it is applied to matters of principle. On the other hand, what people think (whether rightly or wrongly) is a *fact*. Since we are social animals by our very nature, and since, with relatively few exceptions, each of us has to live in society (and we benefit from so living), other people's views should enter into our decision about taking a particular course of action, and if we decide to take it, into the way we undertake it. As in the case of other considerations already mentioned, some parents may feel that guidance as to discretion in such relations may encourage such relations to ensue. Yet, if they think there is a reasonable chance that they will ensue anyway they may feel it appropriate to give some practical guidance about the maintenance of secrecy.

Quite apart from reputation or "scandal," there are two other practical dangers in "unhoused" sexual relations. Perhaps our young people have learned about them sufficiently from the press; but perhaps not, and they should be made aware of them. First, the increasingly frequent instances of assault, abuse or rape of the female partner by third parties in the case of "parking" for lovemaking in dark and remote spots, which, apart from this particular threat, might seem most suitable for effecting discreet sexual activity. The danger of such a possibility represents a responsibility for the male partner. Second, they should beware of what has been a practice of some couples: leaving the motor running in order to keep the heater functioning, and leaving the windows closed; carbon monoxide poisoning has sometimes resulted.

CONCERN FOR THE OTHER

The factors consequent upon premarital sexual relationship that we have already discussed are fairly objective in character. We now turn to a most important factor which to a greater degree involves subjective elements, and which, as far as ethics are concerned, moves to the heart of moral responsibility in interpersonal relations.

8 ✍✍

EMOTIONAL
INVOLVEMENT

We have been discussing ethical responsibility in the context of premarital sex. If we were talking only about prostitution, our task would be completed. But the chances are growing increasingly unlikely that this is the form our young people's premarital sexual experience will take. During the same month the papers of San Francisco reported: (1) in spite of general increase in crime, there was a decrease in rape and prostitution, and (2) there was an increase in unmarried pregnancies. Now the decrease in any form of crime is, on the face of it, a good thing. But taking these two facts together, it is not implausible to conclude that the decrease in rape and in the violation of laws against prostitution is due to the fact that sex is more available outside of these illegal means. These statistics do not suggest that there is a decrease in premarital sexual activity.

EFFECT ON PERSONS

In most instances these days necking, petting, and, finally, sexual intercourse are grounded in a degree of acquaintanceship which at the least is worthy of the label "friendship." Often these intimacies reflect closer ties of affection and emotion. This means that before the act there is generally *something* to express (whether this "something" is adequate to the fullness of the form of expression or not). This very fact means that more than expression is likely to result. Since sex is sacramental in nature and sacramental relationships are more than merely a symbol (an "outward and visible sign") of meaning, it is not only an effect, it is a new cause—a stimulus to inner affection and emotional involvement. This affection and involvement may well continue to grow with continued physical expression and is likely to embrace, in an ever widening circle, other aspects of life and activity.

In marriage, this is the way we want it to be. This is one of the reasons sex should be given a very significant place in the scheme of values in marriage. But the deepening of the relationship may or may not be the intent in the case of the unmarried friendship. Yet, the fact is that sexual intimacy does deepen relationships. This is true of a single occasion—things are never the same thereafter—and of course it is even more true if a pattern of sexual intimacy has developed.

Here we come to the heart of ethical responsibility. We are dealing not with principles and codes but with

93

the direct effects one's decision may have on other persons, for good or for ill. As Martin Buber, the philosopher-theologian, has so well pointed out, our relationship to God is not I–it (in either direction), but I–Thou. Therefore any relationship between one human being and another should be I–Thou: a fundamental moral norm that *persons are not to be treated as things.* The sensitivity to this point which we hope will be engendered in our young people in the area under consideration, will apply to all other aspects of their living in society now and in the years ahead. In order to enhance this effect, not only in regard to sex relationships or any affectional relationships, but in other interpersonal connections as well, it is important that the parents and the young people realize that the detailed explanations next taken up are not to be regarded as a practical survey of "ways and means" in a flatly pragmatic dimension. Rather they are meant to encourage realism in regard to genuine factors which should enter into responsible choices affecting their happiness and the best personal development and welfare of those with whom they will be coming in contact in any degree of relationship.

EFFECT OF SEXUAL COMPATIBILITY

What bearing does sexual compatibility between the given partners have on the causative—as contrasted with the expressive—aspect of sex? It depends. If both parties are relatively experienced and the particular sex connection is markedly unsuccessful, it is true that general affectional relationship may not be deepened by sexual contact; as a matter of fact it may be diminished. But not necessarily; this may represent a challenge to the couple and they may be drawn closer in their continued attempt to make it work out. Or, if one party is experienced and the other is not and the relationship is unsuccessful as to the experienced party, the relationship may not deepen for him; but it may deepen for the inexperienced party who, in not realizing what he or she is missing, may regard the degree of sexual stimulus achieved as very significant. If neither party is experienced or knowledgeable, what they might regard later in their lives as unsuccessful may at the time seem to them quite satisfactory on its own footing and have the effect of creating ever-increasingly close ties.

If the couple is compatible, however, and the result is sexual fulfillment for both, there is no question about the positive bearing the continuance of intimacy will have on the whole relationship. Speaking abstractly about the relation of sex to total personal involvement, this is a good thing; it is quite in line with what sex is supposed to be at its best. It is when we move to the concrete situation that there can be, in given instances, destructive—or, at the least, complicating—results.

DYNAMICS OF SEX RELATIONSHIPS

Discussion with young people in this area should, by all means, avoid mere abstractions. Concrete examples involving dynamic, as contrasted with supposed static, factors should be used, especially "case histories" which will elicit questions for further discussion. If the parents can supply illustrations which come, fully or in part, from personal or vicarious experience (with, of course, anonymity preserved where appropriate), all the better. Should such not be available in the parents' minds, and as an illustration of the type of "case history" which might serve well in this connection, here are three examples:

1. Tom, who takes a liberal view of sex, wants to be free of emotional entanglements. Mary wants to go the whole way with him. He tells her quite frankly that she should not "take it too seriously"; she is not to regard his going ahead as being any commitment to her whatsoever. He goes so far as to warn her not "to fall in love" with him. Let's assume this fits her own mood about the matter, and she rejoices in such perfect understanding as they embark on a course of action that promises to be pleasurable to them both. Time goes on; first unconsciously, and then consciously but unvoiced, there is a steady increase of Tom's affection for Mary, and an increasing dependence on her and her companionship in general, as well as on the intimate relationship. This is not happening to Mary who, looking for a deeper relationship, becomes involved with Bill. The time comes when she feels she is in love with Bill and decides to "cut out" any other relationship. So she begins to drift away from Tom, and she finally tells him that she doesn't want to go on, because he is now in love with someone else.

At this point Tom realizes, if he had not before, that

96

he has gotten "in deep" with Mary, and he suffers a considerable hurt. Mary, of course, on becoming aware of this fact, could say, "Well, a deal is a deal." The kind of relationship which was undertaken was his idea. But this is to look at the fundamental and potentially all-embracing connection in a "contractual" way and overlook the person-to-person existential reality. It would be only under a very wooden ethical theory that Mary could escape a sense of guilt.

2.　Lucille had gone the whole way with two different companions in a sporadic fashion and under circumstances less than conducive to the achievement of her sexual fulfillment, of the nature of which she was not fully aware. She was sufficiently "softened up" by this novitiate that after a very few dates with Joe she entered fully and wholeheartedly into an affair with him. He was a more sophisticated lover than were her other two friends, and also he was able to arrange more conducive surroundings. As a result, for the first time, she experienced orgasm, and more and more she counted on this fulfillment and anticipated it. Here, quite apart from the general broadening and deepening of the relationship, she was specifically "held" by the fact of the reliable outcome of their sexual intimacies. On the other hand, this was not for Joe a new or particularly distinctive experience, and hence he was less held by it. Should Joe begin to concentrate in other directions, perhaps eventually to the exclusion of Lucille, she is bound to feel bereft. She might feel compelled to fill the vacuum, with perhaps not too high a requirement as to the reality or stability of the other levels of relationship with the person selected or accepted. Since girls, especially, do not readily forget any relationship, she may be burdened by the memory of her relationship with Joe in the comparisons she will make in future situations.

3.   Bill, who had been a virgin, became well acquainted with Josephine, a young divorcée several years older than himself. Though it cannot be said that she seduced him, since he was bewitched by the idea of sexual experience, she did make the path easy and he was quite enthralled by the whole thing. She became his teacher and offered a varied curriculum in the full scope of sexual contact. The breakthrough having been made and his own education relatively complete, he now turned, quite naturally, to girls of his own age and found a sense of achievement in instructing others, their initial naïveté being part of the attraction. He began to find less and less time to see Josephine, causing her increasing depression and anxiety.

These examples are not uncommon. They are typical of a wide variety of situations which illustrate the role of sexual expression as a *cause*, and in many instances *the* cause, of a chain reaction.

Place of Fraud and Duress

The illustrations chosen do not include elements of dishonesty or duress, but these can enter the picture too. A male with a conscious objective of sexual conquest may verbally express affection in fuller terms than he is in fact prepared to implement. He can affirm that he "loves" the girl, or that he is "in love" with her, and he may even talk of marriage—when all this is really just a "line." It is true that girls should take "lines" with a grain of salt, but in many instances these are the words they *want* to hear. So they are all too ready to accept them.

On the other hand, the words may be sincere, and even a girl who has been burnt a couple of times is not always able to distinguish the true from the false. Also, a girl who has not been well instructed as to facts that should be taken into account on reaching a No answer, or has not thought too seriously about it (perhaps simply assuming a No answer before marriage), can be quite quickly "taken in" (since her desires may well be working on the side of the persuasive argument) by the reasoning/rationalization of an articulate and winsome companion. If she is not as smart as he is, such an operator is really utilizing a form of duress.

Another form of duress (for practical purposes) obtains when either a boy or a girl has not been accustomed to certain luxuries which the other partner can provide. For example, assuming that the divorcée referred to in illustration 3 had a very attractive apartment, a well-stocked bar and a smart foreign car she readily supplied for the use of her young paramour. Though falling short of actually placing him in a gigolo relationship, she does have the financial ability and willingness to take care of some of his needs. All of this is an additive to the more direct factor of sexual urge. In such cases, it might be hard for the other partner actually to distinguish in his or her mind which factors are more operative in the continuation of the relationship.

What we have suggested are factors other than "inward and spiritual" bases which may enter into the decision to have sexual relationships, and outcomes which may not be predicted (even assuming sincerity and good faith in the beginning) as the relationship progresses.

Awareness of all these factors on the part of a young person is a good thing. He or she may learn them soon enough with experience, although it is better when parents can give them a "preview." The results of this type of instruction may be twofold: (1) the instructee may see them as existential (as contrasted with absolutist) factors to weigh against proceeding to premarital sexual intercourse at all; (2) they may govern in a measure what particular choices are made and what precautions are taken in the course of the relationship. In the case of the latter it would be wise to suggest some "rules of the game" which represent the practical application of the general norm of ethical responsibility in any relationship.

Claims of Honesty

The root and ground of Judeo-Christian ethics are found in justice and love. Prior to the more fragile subjective claims of love is the requirement of plain honesty and fairness. Justice requires that we fulfill the legitimate rights and expectations of the other. Applying this to the field under consideration, the following norms are fundamental:

1.   All "lines" should be ruled out. No one should say, even poetically (since hearers do not always distinguish poetic expression from declaration of fact) more than he means. This is more than a stricture against conscious lying; it calls for conscious thought as to what one really does mean. It is easy for a companion, particularly in romantic circumstances (e.g., after an exciting party, sharing a beautiful view, under the spell of the newness of a friendship, sexual and/or alcoholic stimulus) to "feel" a degree of devotion and to imagine a degree of uniqueness which in fact are not representative of the ongoing attitudes and feelings justified by the actual relationship. Things said and done under such circumstances are often vividly remembered by the partner—even if not by the spokesman.

It is true that one party can, in effect, induce extravagant statements if he or she wants to hear them. He may find his own statements or gestures matched by a partner who, out of kindness, does not want to have him feel "let down." Reticence on the other side, from the most honest motives, can be interpreted as "coldness" or abruptness. Certainly the latter two qualities are neither attractive nor kind; yet there are circumstances in which it would be better to lean over backward in that direction than to go "all out" with statements or actions which are not truly representative of one's feeling in the relationship.

2.   Young people, in mixed company, frequently do talk about sex and about sex ethics. No strictures from parents or others will prevent them from engaging in "bull sessions" or discussion in pairs about these matters, nor would we particularly want to prevent such discussions. Often, such analyses (thought by the analyzers to be quite profound) precede explicit physical relationship. The discussion, whether it has been staged as such or not, has its own softening up role, because people in good health are generally sexually stimulated by talking about sex.

When it comes down to arguing the case for specific action, it is the obligation of the would-be persuader to take into account the question of parity between the parties, the ability of the other to "hold his own." And also there should be some sensing as to whether the other party is really convinced along sound and thoughtful lines or is simply bowled over by the glibness of the persuader. The question, in other words, is not whether he or she "will," but whether he or she really "wants to"—not just at the moment but in terms of a somewhat longer-term view of how life and relationships ought to be organized. An example of such decency would be this comment—not unheard of, "I've thought it through and really think it's all right for us to go ahead. But I really don't believe you feel that way. So let's not—unless and until you really do." (This or any form of similar words, depending upon motivation, can represent a wrong or a right purpose; for example, the last statement could actually be a carefully designed come on!) If the party later decides to go ahead it would be a more deliberate decision, based on the opportunity for thought and weighing, apart from the direct presence of the charm of the partner and the otherwise compelling nature of his arguments. In the eventual outcome of the relationship and its possible side effects, the initiator's conscience will be clear, at least to the extent that the other party made a free and deliberate decision.

3.   Unless there is virtual poverty involved, there naturally would be some "side benefits" to dating, even if only a meal out, breaking the monotony of meals at home; a ride in a car; or companionship for a movie. Having pleasant experiences built into the relationship is not in itself wrong if they fit the means or level of living of the party involved. On the other hand, an inordinate provision of nice things paralleling the proposal of a plan for sexual intimacy is unfair. In fact it ought to be barred on even a self-regarding basis. Because of sheer pride, in this as in other aspects of an affectional connection, a person ought to want to win on his own merits and not "buy" sexual favors by indirection. In any case, this can put pressure—whether recognized or not—on the other party.

These and other such premises are the implications of justice. When the implications of justice and love intermingle, other questions arise.

CLAIMS OF AGAPÉ LOVE

Here we must distinguish between two kinds of love. For them the Greek language has more precise words: *eros* and *agapé*.* *Eros* is the love for another where the source *is* the other. We are attracted because the person is attractive; you love because the person is—to you, at least—lovable. *Agapé* is often intermingled with *eros* in practice, but it is isolatable in situations, or at times, where the other party is not particularly lovable or attractive, or is no longer so in the eyes of the lover. Whether operating along with the genuine *eros* love or separately (under given circumstances), it comes into play when the other party is in *need* of concern, attention and care. Its most fundamental cause or stimulus is the recognition that this is the way that God loves us—not because we are lovable or attractive necessarily, but because we need to be accepted and to be met as we are. Fundamental in the Judeo-Christian tradition is the belief that God is like that toward us and wants us to be like that toward others. The conscious or unconscious response to God's love is being like that toward others.† Many a person who never heard of the word *agapé*, or for that matter, has had no visible connection with the Church, has displayed this kind of love. But presumably it would be more apparent in a society deeply influenced by Judeo-Christianity and even more so where there is a more specific

* A third kind of love, *philia*, is not directly relevant here. For a discussion of it, and a fuller treatment of *eros* and *agapé*, see my *Doing the Truth*.

† The most terse statement in this connection is 1 John 4:11: "Beloved, if God so loved us, we also ought to love one another." (RSV)

conscious intake of the source of this love.* In any case, in specifying some of the ethical obligations flowing from our general obligation to love other people, we are not talking about liking other people, but about the obligation to meet the needs of others, especially in the context of established relationships.

Awareness Quite apart from whether one ought or ought not to have entered into a particular relationship, if the relationship is a *fact*, it is important that each party in it be sensitive to what is really happening to the other party. This involves awareness in greater depth than simply the hearing of words or participation in actions. This applies at all points in the time span of the relationship. Nothing remains static, particularly people's emotions, feelings and attitudes toward those with whom they have close connection. For example, often in the fear of losing the partner, one will "keep a stiff upper lip" and purport to see their relationship as joyous when in fact it is quite depressing. It is also possible for one party to read into what the other is saying or writing (in the case of correspondence) more than is intended or than the realities of the situation could justify. When there is discussion of the relationship, either calmly or quarrelsomely, it is important to seek to sense what the other party is *really saying*, not merely what words and phrases are being emitted.

Candor If, in the mind and affections of one party,

* This is doubtless one reason—perhaps the principal reason—that couples active together in a given religious tradition have a much higher percentage of marital success, at least as judged by divorce statistics. See, *e.g.*, my *If You Marry Outside Your Faith* (New York: Harper & Row, 1962), ch. 2.

the relationship is "dying on the vine," it is naturally difficult for him to articulate the fact, and often the fact is withheld as part of supposed kindness to the other. Delay, however, may rob the other party of opportunities for affection elsewhere, or allow him to "get in deeper"—thus contributing to greater frustration and hurt later on. If one party has doubts about the relationship or is already emotionally involved with someone else, it is not really serving the need of the other to continue mouthing sentiments which are well-meant but no longer fully true. In such situations it is difficult when confronted with the question, "Do you love me with your whole heart," to say, "No, I don't." Yet a reassuring affirmation, while doubtless comforting at the moment, will lead to a greater letdown later than would some kind and careful words indicating reservations.

Care about inequity of relationships   Related to the above, and overlapping with it, is the need for attention to the dynamics of the situation. As far as may be perceived, perhaps both have begun a relationship with the same level of *eros*, at least of mutual interest and satisfaction. For example, both may have articulated the context of a "light" affair by words such as "fun" and "we enjoy it." But quite apart from whether the degree of inward and spiritual involvement makes sexual intimacy appropriate, if such is in fact undertaken there should be sensitivity to the signs of development of greater depth in the other party; for example, increase in worry about apparent neglect

106

on the part of the other, increasing claims on time, and increasing pressure towards exclusivity. Any one of these warning signs can be met, or satisfied. But where he is heading with the other person cannot be so easily met if there is insensitivity as the trend develops. If the whole relationship has reached greater breadth and depth, a certain degree of commitment comes to be assumed. If one party is no longer able to come through on the particular level of commitment in the present and/or the future, the most thoughtful and responsible strategy is to face how to "lighten up" the situation or withdraw from it entirely—in the interests of both. An abrupt break is cruel; equally cruel is sliding along down a dead-end street, when things will be brought to a stop anyway. The balancing of these likely hurts, proper timing and choice of words (expressing genuine reality in relation to the now and the prospective future situation) are called for. It is almost too obvious to say that getting out of an affair is harder than getting into one. It does need to be said to young people, who may well run the gamut, that they are likely to have a lot of crises and that care for the outcome should be kept in mind from the start, affecting all that is said and done throughout.

LIKELY EFFECT OF THESE CONSIDERATIONS

Talking to young people about these aspects of emotional relationships generally receives attentive and responsive reaction. Even if they have grown diffident or rebellious about parental, ecclesiastical or societal "don't," they generally want to feel that they are moral persons. Under these circumstances, even without tutelage and often with some naïveté and sentimentality, they profess—however inarticulately—an ethic centering around sincerity and being kind to people. In this, they are not entirely missing the mark. Concern for people, of course, is the heart of Judeo-Christian ethics, quite apart from the validity of given do's and don'ts; even if the latter does not have appeal, the former will have.

A mature analysis of the implications of justice and love in sexual activity will help to elevate natural motivations from the level of mere sentiment and good intentions, and will present young people with the realities he or she will likely be confronting, should such relationships ensue.

In the case of young people who are firm in their intention of abstinence, and who wish to persevere in it until marriage, much of what has been said above is applicable to various degrees of emotional involvement with members of the opposite sex, even when there is no intimacy or limited intimacy. The depth of boy-girl relationships is only affected in a matter of degree by the extent of physical contact. But, true as this is, perennial human experience has demonstrated that the intensity of relationship and thus the risk of mounting insecurity with deep hurt are parallel with the increased joy and pleasure occurring when the parties go "the whole way" and continue there. If a couple has decided to go ahead, it is to be hoped that the fruit of the kind of advice suggested in these pages will be a happier outcome—or at least a less unhappy outcome —in a given relationship. On the other hand, it may be that a realistic coverage of all these possibilities may in itself discourage the young person from proceeding at all, even if he takes a pragmatic rather than absolute view of ethical restraint. If this is the case, the young person will be better off in terms of mental health than the one who has accepted a No on a negative or an absolutist basis. The latter may represent suppression of desire and this may be very unfortunate for future sexual maturity, whereas the practice of restraint based on an existential analysis of likely outcomes with given confrontations, will result not in suppression, but rather in a healthy recognition of the reality of sexual interest which will contribute to the prospects of healthy emotional development.

Try it once?   A third attitude is possible. Natural curiosity, particularly when stirred by recounting of actual—or wishful-thinking—activities by members of the peer group, may result in a decision to "try it once." It may be decided, in connection with a given friendship or love, that it would be a good thing if they found out "what it's like." Coupled with this can be an actually sincere intent not to do it again. If one could be sure that it would work out this way, this might in itself not be particularly harmful—in fact, arguments could be put forth to support the idea. However, here the greater experience of the parents (personal or vicarious) should supply an amber light. The effect of the sexual act is not something external to the person, like playing "the slots" once in passing through a Nevada town, or seeing what bridge and poker are like. Sex is so deep a drive (and is meant to be) involving the mind and spirit, that in its compulsion to repetition it is more nearly analogous to alcoholism and narcotics addiction. (I would like to emphasize that I am using these analogies in relationship to their compulsive aspects only, and do not wish to connect the ethics and aesthetics of those addictions to the sexual experience.)

A person is not an alcoholic when he can drink once and let it alone, or drink with measured restraint. But the person whose psychological and/or physical make-up is, in fact, alcoholic cannot, with safety, take *one* drink. It is not that this particular intake is harmful in itself, but it so readily softens him up for the second and the latter markedly adds to this process, leading him to the third, *ad infinitum* (or *ad finitum*). Even more marked is the illustration of narcotics addiction. One shot of heroin can so readily lead to the second, third, and fourth, and by that time the individual is really "hooked."

These analogies represent more definite and crucial trends than are true in the case of sex, but they are genuine analogies. It is easy, in advance of any sexual experience or a sexual act with a given person, sincerely to intend that it be "once-and-that's-all." But such a design fails to take into account the new force which is the fruitage of actually engaging in the act.

110

Assuming the experiment is enjoyable and successful, all the greater will be the desire to repeat it. But if, due to immaturity or unpropitious surroundings, it is not successful, the idea will not necessarily be dropped. In fact, there are many parents and other persons concerned with the well-being of young people who would not be particularly pleased about an unhappy outcome to such an experiment, if the experiment must be. Here, a new stimulus enters: the search for success. The result may be additional attempts. And then, with success, there is the stimulus already referred to, more powerful than advance contemplation of it would indicate.

All of the foregoing has been written on the unexpressed premise that the person being advised has the full use of his faculties and is really free to "make up his mind." This is not likely to be so, to the fullest extent in any case. But the possibility of such freedom can be thwarted by a specific factor in modern life, one which has been looming ever larger in recent decades, namely, alcohol.

9 ✍✍

ALCOHOL AND SEX

Paralleling the increasing sexual freedom of young people is their increasing use of alcohol. They drink more, they drink longer, they drink harder, and they drink sooner. It is no longer "the occasional glass of wine with the family at dinner." Curfews are later and later—in many places nonexistent. The "proof" of the liquor is up, there has been a marked transition from beer to vodka. More often than not, drinking begins now in the middle years of high school rather than in the middle years of college, as was more common in previous generations.

This changing phenomenon in our society creates a variety of problems and raises a number of significant questions which are not within the scope of this book to discuss. This is not a treatise on alcohol or alcoholism; nor is the author taking advantage of the reader's attention up to this point to deliver a "temperance talk."

But a direct connection between the use of alcohol and teen-age sex makes it necessary for the counselor —parental or otherwise—to include consideration of alcohol if the picture is to be whole and realistic.

There are two connections between the subjects. One is the deliberate use of alcohol in connection with sexual activity—actual or contemplated; and the other is the unintended effect on sexual decisions resulting from the use of alcohol for its own sake. But before either can be discussed in a balanced way with young people, it is important that we help them toward a sound understanding of the place of alcohol in life.

GOOD/EVIL

Most people drink these days and the percentage of drinkers in the population is steadily rising. More and more young people are drinking and are beginning at earlier ages, and their opportunity to drink is constantly increasing. As we have seen in the area of sex (and it is true of most other areas of activity, too) a flat parental No is not very effective. Anyway, fewer and fewer parents are themselves "dry" and their example would belie any words about abstinence they might be inclined to utter. A negative declaration on the part of parents is likely to have the effect of enhancing their young people's decision to experiment in this area. A negative is unsound anyway—and I speak as a nondrinker.

What it is important to communicate is a healthy

basis for decision-making in regard to the drinking
that is likely to occur, beginning at one age or another.
Alcohol is one of the good things in life, one of God's
gifts, developed through the mind of man. It has a
number of +'s. To most people drinks taste good. But
more than that they can make the drinker "feel" good.
Tensions are relieved, the "warmer" aspects of personality come to the fore, shyness is in part conquered,
self-confidence is buttressed, social and interpersonal
capacities are enhanced, articulation and self-revela-
tion promoted. Nothing new is added to the personality, there is simply a heightening of certain aspects of what is already there.

All this presupposes moderate and spaced intake. Excess can do severe things:

1. While heightening the facets mentioned,
   drinking can "dim out" (like a rheostat) other
   balancing personal facets and thus distort perspective. What begins as emphasizing of reality
   can pass into unreality or even fantasy.

2. Destructively depressed, hostile or other anti-
   social facets of personality can come to the fore.
   Again, nothing new is added but the least constructive and least attractive aspects in a person can become dominant.

3. Self-confidence can become unrealistic overconfidence; the ego can become all too central,
   with undisciplined aggressiveness. Or, alterna-

tively, self-depreciation, withdrawal into one-self, can ensue.

4. Malfunction can result: physical incapacity or, more important to our main topic, inability to make balanced decisions.

All this—the +'s of moderate intake and the —'s of excessive drinking—is true of persons of all ages. But with teen-agers there is greater likelihood that another factor will be present: immaturity. And this element affects the picture in two ways: (a) less balance when intoxicated, and (b) less awareness of the dangers of excess quantity and less watchfulness as to intake especially due to the pressure of conformity to the pattern of companions in the peer group.

Thus, quite apart from one's attitude toward drinking in general, there is sound practical reason behind parental and other prohibitions against drinking before a given age, comparable to minimum age requirement for driving licenses. But since our young people will be reaching an age where drinking is permissible, and in many cases will in fact be drinking earlier, it is important to cover some of these above points (some of which will be obvious to many of them through observation of their parents' behavior) in the hope that when they *do* drink the effects may not be complicated by unwarranted guilt feeling about drinking, and that a pattern of moderation may be established early. At the same time instruction as to the signs of incipient alcoholism is important, a matter discussed later.

Now back to the direct bearing of alcohol, particularly excessive drinking, on sex, using the distinction made above: intentional use of alcohol in relation to sex and unintended results of the mixing of the two.

INTENTIONAL MIXING OF ALCOHOL AND SEX

For some, drinking is deliberately instrumental to one of several objectives:

1. The user has learned, either from his own experience or from that of others, that one or two drinks will relieve shyness of approach—due to either the user's personality or his inexperience —or will help remove the vestiges of inhibition.
2. The user figures that alcohol will "soften up" a date toward a cooperative answer (making her more receptive to his "line," his arguments for going ahead) and lessen her reservations about coition.
3. He may believe that what transpires in the fore-play (which may turn out to be the *only* play) and in the full act may be, with alcohol, more exciting, more fully sensuous. He feels *both* parties will be more "lost" in it and more "themselves."

116

There is a factual basis for each of these assumptions, but there is an important reservation as to the third: If he has too much to drink he may find himself temporarily impotent, particularly in a new situation with the unfamiliarity and the uncertainty which can accompany it. Or, if he is able to begin coition, he may in the course of it lose his erection.

In reading the above, it might be taken for granted that deliberate use of alcohol is something the male of the species engages in; these days, however, girls use alcohol for the same purposes—with more emphasis on the alleviation of a sense of guilt. There are girls who regularly drink beforehand, sometimes for a fictional purpose: afterwards they can feel that the reason they yielded is that they were drinking, having had no real doubt all along that they would yield! While in the case of a girl impotence does not occur, she can, with too much drink, become numb to the whole thing, unable to reach orgasm, disinterested, or even surly. Therefore, the man who is seeking to ply his date with liquor can overshoot his mark.

What do we have to say to all this? To "recap" what has been said, most parents may not want their young people to drink at all. But in any case, all should be concerned with the use of alcohol on the part of immature people, both because of the possible development of patterns that may later flower into chronic alcoholism, and because of the effects on the days and nights they are now living. Even those who feel that

117

teen-agers should be free to drink or have given up any hope of preventing them from drinking should be concerned with the effects of their deliberate use of alcohol in connection with contemplated sexual activity.

First, whatever moral theory is right, a young person should not proceed to sexual relations unless his conscience is clear—in general, and with reference to the particular relationship contemplated. He should not be using a chemical to fill the gap between the moral grounding for his decision and the action itself. If it takes alcohol to enable him to proceed without a sense of guilt, he should not be proceeding at all.

Second, if—rightly or wrongly—he is fully ready to go ahead without the need of alcohol, it is not fair that he fill the gap between the partner's degree of reticence and her giving in by a less-than-human causation. None but the most amoral or jaded would seek to gain his ends by use of a knockout drop or a chemical aphrodisiac, or by force or duress. The use of alcohol for this purpose is actually of the same moral category. It is a deliberate limitation of the freedom of decision of the other party.

Third, the theory as to the place of alcohol in improving the joy of sex is not entirely well-grounded. It is an ambivalent addition in any case. There are those who feel they want to be fully "there"—therefore sober; alcohol can numb and obscure as well as highlight the manifold possibilities of feeling and response. In any case, to the degree that a certain amount

of alcoholic saturation magnifies a stimulus and response, there is danger of a distortion of the place of
the sensuous (itself a good thing in life) in the whole
picture of things. And even those who do not wish to
say an absolute No to unmarried sex should want to
keep it in proper perspective as to the whole development of personality and not have it magnified out of
proportion, in terms of priorities and individual decisions. And if, as suggested above, the quantity of intake is such as to create impotence—and the frustration, self-searching, and sense of inferiority arising
from even a single incident of this character—the
result can be either withdrawal from contemplated
future approaches, or vice versa: an overcompensation
by way of additional "tries" with less discrimination.

So here we have some pragmatic reasons to present
on the side of sobriety in connection with dating where
there is the intention (or hope) of sexual intimacy.
If the counselor believes in a pattern of total abstinence,
the reasons above are apt to be more convincing to a
young person than pronouncement of a dictate against
all drinking under any and all circumstances, and if
the parent happens to be "liberal," the spelling out of
such considerations can be persuasive toward moderation.

UNINTENDED EFFECTS OF ALCOHOL

Young people today often confront us with a different situation. Without the two consciously linked in
their minds, they may be intending both drinking and

sex. Or more specifically, they may already have established a habit of social drinking and are beginning to think about sexual activity, either in general or with a particular person. Even apart from any instrumental use of alcohol in the matter, it may well play a part in the outcome.

1. Suppose that, due to parental influence or otherwise, the young persons have actually decided No. Assume they drink to a degree of intoxication. The natural excitation of the other's presence can lead, in the mind of one or the other, to a reopening of the question. At this point, the positive factors hitherto regarded as outweighed, may seem to have particular weight, or rationalizations may spontaneously arise (alcohol often does stimulate the imagination). A decision may be made then and there, by one or both, to go ahead, especially if sexual feelings have already been heightened by a degree of kissing, necking, and petting. If one of the partners has not, even under the influence of alcohol, gone so far in his or her thinking, resistance is obviously weakened and feelings and/or desire to please more easily dominate the previously-held convictions.

2. Particularly vulnerable in this regard is the young person who has not accepted absolutes but who (either in line with his parents' views or contrary to them) has decided to take an existential, but responsible, view of the whole matter, and to weigh all the factors connected with each particular decision. It is obvious, even to the point of being a cliché, that in this

120

realm (as in all realms of life), weighing of values is affected by excessive drinking. There can be a distortion of the value properly attached to various factors (such evaluation is difficult enough when one is sober). This can be pinpointed a little more:

a. The rosiness achieved tends to give greater force to the here-and-now and tends to deflate the relevance of the future.

b. Features previously regarded as relevant in any weighing have their edges beveled, with possible negative outcomes seeming easier to handle.

c. The particular relationship can appear to have a heightened significance and more basis for depth than it really has, and thus seem to be more worthy of full physical expression than it might seem to be in sobriety.

Even basic views toward the matter may change. We have seen how a youth, who has accepted an absolute, can move to a relativistic ethic while under the stimulus of alcohol. So, too, one who has already taken an existential stance—but a responsible one—may with sufficient alcohol decide for what he would not label as a hedonist approach, but which, in fact, is; namely, that anything goes: a simple "I do what I want to do." Here we are talking of young people who would seriously make decisions in the area of sex before committing themselves to a particular course of action. With this existential attitude, all the more *should they safeguard their freedom to make responsible decisions.*

Further, no matter how enlightened they may feel their view is, it is difficult to avoid guilt-feelings in a culture in which there is such a strong residuum of the conventional morals. We should certainly point out to them the danger of guilt-feelings with regard to present happiness and the formation of the conscious and unconscious personality in the future, and we should stress the importance of their making decisions in such a way that they will feel free of guilt in having made them. Adding alcohol to the picture almost guarantees that distortion will enter into the decision-making and as a result they will be less able afterwards to be at peace about what they have done. In the cold light of day they may realize, for example, that they really didn't care all that much about the partner. They may even feel that they are in no particular mood to carry through with the relationship on the other levels implied by the words said and actions done. It is one thing for a person to get involved with his eyes open and another to slip into intimacy and have to face the implications of the act, no matter how joyous it was at the time or is in memory.

There is another factor. Once sex has been experienced, there is an almost automatic change in the weighing operation. Such weighing cannot be, and should not be, so "cool" that excluded from the factors is the expectation of joy of the act itself. This is a positive good, whether or not it is outweighed by negative factors. But if a person has gone ahead and if the experience has been successful, or relatively successful, future weighing will include the knowledge of the joy of the act. This is a stronger force than the contemplation of it, and thus can add considerably to the outbalancing of sound negative factors.

Even if a person's conviction, mentally speaking, is unchanged about an absolute No, the actual experience, particularly during the years when the degree of stimulus is (quite naturally) high, can have an almost compulsive effect on the future. This may result in either of two things:

1. Continuation of the physical relationship with his first partner, which experience shows can outlast the natural life of the friendship. Such a continuity can narrow the scope of his entering into or appreciating the personalities of others. It can in fact deepen a bond which otherwise might not have deepened, and which, on other grounds, it might not be wise to deepen. In short, he gets in deeper and deeper.

2. Frenetic seeking of partners in an ever widening circle, with less and less concern for the meaningfulness of the relationship which the sexual act is supposed to represent; and finally, the erasing in consciousness of the sense of the importance of significant personal connection as a prerequisite to sexual expression.

Either of these outcomes may well have taken the person quite a way beyond his original thoughtful intentions, and in either case, something serious has happened. First, it is one thing for a total relationship to develop in depth along all lines, with or without sexual expression; it is another for this to happen as the compulsive repetition of sexual connection. Second, it is one thing for a person to accept a hedonist attitude toward sex, with promiscuity as the actual or desired pattern; it is another thing to slip into this pattern unwittingly.

So much for the effects, intended or unintended, of alcohol upon patterns of relationship. Alcohol also affects the exercise of responsibility in connection with sexual relationships.

1. The importance of care about birth control has been emphasized. But this is the very thing that alcohol reduces. We are not here talking about the morals of particular sexual activity, but rather of the moral responsibility to exercise birth control in any case. Assume that full coitus was uncontemplated, in that neither party had come equipped. Intoxicated (in greater or lesser degree) the couple may now proceed anyway. Even if *coitus interruptus* or *coitus reservatus* is intended, unexpected orgasm may take the couple by surprise. With enough to drink a devil-may-care attitude may have possessed the couple creating an overconfidence as to the chances of getting by without complete caution. There may even be a rapid computation under the rhythm method; but careful mathematics calls for sobriety. Of course one or the other may have come equipped with a contraceptive device. But in the case of heavy drinking they may not bother

to take advantage of it or take proper care as to placement of it.

2.   Overdrinking will probably diminish watchfulness as to the danger of disease, in the case of young people of a promiscuous bent. An intoxicated girl is less likely to check the signs of venereal disease in a new partner; and an intoxicated boy will be more relaxed about the need of prophylactic protection.

3.   Whether or not a given unmarried liaison should occur, if it does there is responsibility for discretion as to time and place in order not to create collateral harm to either party or to others. It is obvious that drinking can add to impulsiveness. And it can numb awareness of even fairly obvious risks and create diffidence as to care for what otherwise would be observed as precautions.

4.   Alcohol produces insensitivity as to the interpersonal factors in the relationship which have been discussed in the preceding chapter. For example: affirming no more than one really means is difficult enough when sober; it is virtually impossible when drunk; sensing where the partner really is in degree of involvement calls for a maximum of discernment, and therefore relative sobriety.

THE IMPORTANCE OF ALCOHOL EDUCATION

All of these points can be made with more effectiveness if in the instruction a floor is put under them, namely, basic coverage of the operation of alcohol in

the human system. This is important as part of the
education of young people in any case; and perhaps
a thorough job will have been done in his school or
Church youth group. But it is important for a parent
to see to it that this fundamental education has been
communicated before the possibility of heavy drinking
may be a threat, and—with reference to the concern
of this book—a confusing and distorting, even blind-
ing, factor in the young person's decision-making
about sex.

To aid a parent in this regard, or for direct reading
by the young person himself, a number of manuals or
pamphlets are available. Some of these are listed in
the bibliography.

10 ✎✎

TOWARD MARRIAGE

This work is not intended as a marriage manual nor as a text for marriage counselors. There are a good number of books in this field. Some very useful ones are listed in the bibliography.

An obvious time for careful and full marriage counseling is when a particular marriage is contemplated. These days more and more clergy are providing marriage counseling sessions for engaged couples; for example, such counseling is required by the canon law of the Episcopal Church.* Counseling in which the instruction is of wider scope is provided by various agencies in some cities. Happily, more and more couples contemplating marriage are taking advantage of these opportunities.†

* Canon 17, § 2.

† Since such facilities are under varying sponsorship in different localities, it would be well to make inquiry of your family doctor or of the office of the local Community Fund or Health and Welfare Council.

On the other hand, marriage counseling without reference to a particular marriage in view may seem irrelevant and perhaps have limited impact. But the very treatment of the proper and improper use of sex necessarily involved in discussions with teen-agers means that some reference to marriage is inevitable. And analysis of marriage at this point is in one way even more important: it can have more effective bearing on the choice of a potential spouse than discussion of the matter when the decision has been made or virtually made.

In general conversation in the middle and late teens it is natural for the subject of marriage to come up. There are many opportunities to say something which would be relevant during that period and during the years that follow, particularly on the question of entering into a more abiding affection which might lead to marriage or of actual focusing upon a particular person as a potential life partner. Also this is a good time to bring sound influence (hopefully) on the formation of attitudes toward sex within marriage.

It is not easy to answer the question: Why do John and Mary decide to get married? Yet such decisions are not made out of the blue. They are grounded in and influenced by the values and priority scales which have already developed in each person. Presumably reactions to parents, their marriage, the marriages of family friends and of the parents of their peer group, and the standards of their peer group, all have their share of influence. Then, on the assumption that dialogue between the parents and teen-agers is of some value (on this assumption has this book been written), it is not unlikely that this, too, will have some place in the formation and development of norms of choice.

This does not imply that parents can—or should—direct their young people as to whom they should marry. Nor should they attempt to provide a "job description," listing characteristics, achievements, capabilities, and elements of personality, a checklist by which any contemplated marriage of one of their own should be judged. Further, parents should be prepared for the fact that in spite of all they say in advance or say at the time, the choice of a spouse ultimately will not be their decision, and indeed may be quite contrary to any decision they might have made had they been given the chance (for example, as in some other cultures).

Even as to what may be said we are on very subjective ground, since any parent is bound to reflect what he has found—or feels that he has failed to find—in his own marriage; the parent is bound to reflect his own scheme of values as well. Yet there is much to be said that will be general enough to apply to all parents and all young people. Therefore at the risk of appearing platitudinous we will attempt certain observations in the nature of premises, which have to do with the process and effects of selection in the face of actual specific romantic attachment.

129

WHAT YOU ARE = WHAT YOU'LL CHOOSE

The trouble with some marriages that appear to be "on the rocks" is not that the aggrieved partner did not get what he or she wanted; rather, he did get what he wanted—but at the time he made the choice, he wanted the wrong things. The most significant factor in the actual choice of a mate is what oneself is. If a girl's main interest is momentary pleasure and the means to continue to have it, and if she has little interest in serious subjects or in the responsible aspects of life, she may fall in love with a man who cares for little more than pleasure and who has the means to provide it, even though he may be lacking in other interests or drives. This in the end will probably mean unstable marriage or family life. If a boy is selfish in makeup and shows little awareness of the needs or interests of other people, he may find just such a girl attractive, particularly because of her attraction to him and her devotion, though she shows little sign of serious concerns. The trouble is that one partner may, with maturity and the increase of responsibility, begin to emphasize more serious values, while the other partner does not change. The end result: increasing alienation, growing malaise in the marriage and family life.

Therefore one of the best protections against unsound marriage is a serious and self-critical look at oneself during the teen years, in order to establish the values, attitudes, and responses which, in a measure, would be characteristic of responsible adult life. This, apart from its own value, will to a degree provide the yardstick by which a young person may, consciously or unconsciously, measure persons of the opposite sex with whom he is in contact, as he grows more "serious."

It is not just a question of putting mind over emotion. Emotion generally arises when one sees in another person values and aspirations that he admires and wants to share. On the other hand, no young person should be encouraged to grow serious about one of the opposite sex who might well have all the elements which would seem to match his own mental image if, at the same time, the emotions are not drawn toward the person. Marriage is not just like the choosing of an important employee or a business partner. Essential is the centrifugal force known as love (more specifically, *eros*), especially in the light of the increasing centrifugal forces in our increasingly "scattering" culture. The chances that love will be directed toward the person who will make a good partner are much greater if one knows one's own values, if one knows the other's values, if the values match, and if the values are sound for long-term living.

THE PLACE OF RELIGION

Most persons are likely to have more stability in values and have in themselves a source of minimizing the destructive results of anxiety if they are consciously motivated by active religious faith. Statistics and experience show that a strong factor in a foundation for a stable and fruitful marriage is involvement together in the same religious tradition. This is not simply an unexplainable miracle nor is it based on some crude notion of a "reward" from God (on a *quid pro quo* basis) for doing things for God in the Church. In the couple's joint religious allegiance some quite discernible factors are operative:

1. They are together entering into the Source of *agapé* love, which is a basic support of their marriage relationship (and, one might add, of any interpersonal relationship).

2. In the services of the Church, in the preaching, and in the parish's educational program there is much being communicated, to the unconscious as well as to the conscious level, which nourishes sound personal attitudes having a direct bearing on the capacity to be a good marriage partner.

3. A "tie-in" with a group of other persons committed to the same world-view and influenced (or influenceable) by the same motivations is supportive to the marriage relationship itself.

4. Involvement in the "cause" of the Church is a very wholesome tie for the spouses.

5. When children come along there is a common basis of parental influence in the development of their world-view and ethical values.

132

Religious motivation operating privately in each of the partners can of course be of value; but of much greater value is open and jointly held—and acted out—allegiance.

MIXED MARRIAGES

We live in a pluralistic society and the intermingling of persons of varying religious background—and of none—is increasing all the time. This in itself is a good thing generally in our culture. As this trend increases there is an even greater likelihood that young people will be developing friendships and affections with persons of different religious traditions from their own and with persons with no religious background. Valuable as a common religious commitment in marriage is, it is impossible—even if it were wise—for parents to lay down an absolute rule limiting their young people to association with persons of the same faith. On the other hand, it is wise at the teen-age level of instruction to implant a recognition of the value of marriage with a person of one's own faith. Not only should the positive values of this factor of unity in a marriage be covered, but also the possibility of contention, or at least of tension, in a "mixed marriage," particularly in regard to decisions about the religious upbringing of the children. While children cannot be directed to focus their interest and affections exclusively upon fellow-members of their own Church there are two positive factors which can work to this end:

133

1. Increasingly solid and mature religious faith (there are more mixed marriages on the part of persons who are relatively indifferent to any religious tradition, including their own).

2. Involvement in youth activities under the auspices of the Church.

Neither can be forced, but there can be encouragement and help along this line. The best help is parental example, especially if parental attitudes and behavior in general have won the respect of the children all along and if the parents are capable of openness (this can be wholesome in itself) in the articulation of religious doubts and in seeking truth. At some point it would be well to have the young people read a book on mixed marriages—in advance of their beginning to make choices among their young friends. (Two such books are listed in the bibliography.) Also it can be suggested that when there are any signs of seriousness in the conversations between the "lovers," religion should be included so that there may be an early awareness of the situation. It is astonishing—but a fact —that sometimes couples have fallen in love and even talked about marriage, without either one even *knowing* what the other's religious affiliation is (this does suggest a lack of depth both in their relationship and in their religion!). For many such the only problem thought to be connected with mixed marriages is the wedding (which in itself is not the main problem, especially since virtually all Churches recognize as valid the marriages conducted by ministers of other Churches). When love, or conviction about love, is fully developed then it may be too late, but not always. Sometimes at this point the couple can be moved to give fresh and mature thought to where each stands religiously, in the hope that they may agree (not for each other's sake, but on a basis of conviction) on the same religious tradition. But it is much better that a program toward this end be entered into quite early in the relationship. This is more likely when discussion of religion is part of the couple's general sharing all along.

PARENTS AND CHOOSING

The role of the parents in decisions about specific engagements or marriages contemplated by their children would, by and large, take us beyond the age level with which we are concerned in this book. But our scope here takes us to the very edge of this question. Hence the relevance of these few remarks about the wider role of parents in the choice of a mate on the part of a son or daughter.

Since parents are, and should be, concerned about the welfare of their children—not only as children, but for the rest of their lives—in other regards (e.g., they are quite properly concerned about their children's health, about their educational preparation for a career, etc.), it is quite natural that parents should be concerned about how their children come out in marriage. They rejoice when they see one of their children showing serious interest in someone whom they like (to put it at the lowest level) and whom they feel would make a good partner and it is not surprising that they will seek to encourage such relationships. At the same time, it is understandable that they might be concerned negatively as they see particular relationships developing. But if they are wise they will realize that they are not the ones to choose a marriage partner for any one of their children and that any tendencies manifested in this regard will be resented, and understandably so, by the average young person. Thus there are a few parental roles which call for very careful balance. The vigorous endorsement of a particular prospect or a blatant denunciation of him may—in each case—have results exactly opposite those desired, and at the same time may threaten or sever any relationship productive of sound influence, between parents and the youth. A good guide: Awareness, interest, candor—but "the light touch."

IS ENGAGEMENT A GREEN LIGHT?

The place of the feeling of love in the young person's decision making has been mentioned. What about the role of sex? This book is primarily a book on "premarital sex" in the customary usage of the phrase, where the middle term ("marital") is really irrelevant; what is meant is sexual activity of single persons. Now we turn to premarital sex in the literal sense of the phrase: the question of sexual intimacy between two particular persons contemplating marriage to each other.

However great the growing incidence of sexual activity among young persons in general, it has been fairly common throughout history, especially in particular cultures or subcultures, to "jump the gun" in the case of engagement. In fact pregnancy therefrom often sets the date.

The higher incidence of this situation does not automatically provide a different ethical principle for it. The answer in a given context will still depend, first, on the choice between the two current theories of morality. The conventional view still yields a No. Yet in the mores even those affirming the clean-cut "Thou shalt not" tend to be less judgmental about intercourse in the case of engaged couples—especially after the sexual intimacy (with or without pregnancy) has been ratified by actual marriage. On the other hand, under "the new morality" the need of weighing and the factors to weigh are still there, but the weight of each pro and con will be affected by the fact of engagement—and there are some additional factors; there is certainly no automatic Yes.

On the + side can be weighed the likely joy of *now* fulfillment. They can share in this after marriage, to be sure; but they are living now, not next year.

Some feel that on the + side should be counted the value of finding out in advance whether or not there is sexual compatibility (the plausible assumption being that if there is not, the engagement should be terminated—avoiding at least a potentially crippled marriage). There is obviously some truth in this. But, *per contra*, except under the most unusual circumstances, such a "trial marriage" does not provide a true test. Of course it will probably establish that the couple can, broadly speaking, function sexually, and that they like it; but this can, with a fair degree of safety, be assumed anyway. However, the *modus operandi* of sexual adjustment, while part of the science of physiology and the art of choreography, is much more than this. Also important are (1) external factors such as surroundings, uninterrupted time and continuity of opportunity for the spirit to "blow where it listeth" as to the choice of occasions and modes of intimacy; (2) the contextual factor of sharing and mutual responsibility in the other significant aspects of relationship, and (3) internal factors, such as a good measure of security about the contemplated future, freedom of both parties from guilt-feelings about physical relationships (and remember here the societal and/or parental effects on the unconscious mind), and freedom from fear that it may not work out—itself a negative causative factor (inside or outside marriage).

Some will argue on the — side: he won't respect you if you let him go ahead. *This* point isn't worth much weight; if he was the initiator or an equal partner in the decision and then reacts that way he's either using this point as an "out" otherwise motivated, or he is displaying a patent unfairness that should flash

138

at least an amber light on the road to marriage with him at all.

There is another negative worth weighing: true engagement means commitment to marry. But the very fact that "broken engagement" is a familiar phrase points to the fact that in the greater closeness and exclusivity symbolized by the engagement ring one or another supposed $+$ can turn out to be a 0 or a $-$. And such revelation can be fortunate indeed: it gives a chance, in advance of the assumption of the greater challenge of marriage, to evaluate and perhaps accept the given 0 or $-$, or to call the whole thing quits. If the latter, better earlier than later. Now, granted sexual compatibility is one of the counted on $+$'s (in some cases it can be found to be a 0 or a $-$), in this particular $+$ there is a difference (even if only of degree), especially if the trial proves to be relatively successful (or seemingly so to a couple who have not had previous direct knowledge of complete fulfillment). Sex can be a vivid and all encompassing experience and to the degree it is a proven or supposed $+$ it can blind the couple to possible significant lacks in other aspects of the relationship which would otherwise reveal themselves. To expect this not to be the case presupposes a considerable degree of balance and maturity. In most cases, this presupposes a lot.

On the other hand, it is of course a plain fact that in many, many cases (perhaps in the case of the instructing parents) marriages where coition had preceded the wedding bells have turned out well. And usually there is no real (or even verbalized) regret as to the matter. But this generalization (to the degree that it is true) does not obviate the moral responsibility of conscientious weighing of all the relevant factors in each case. As in every other type of situation an existentialist ethic (if it is really ethic, not just existential) calls for the exercise of more conscientious responsibility than does adherence to a conventional code.

SELECTED
BIBLIOGRAPHY

AMERICAN MEDICAL ASSOCIATION. (Sex Education Series.) Lerrigo and Southard, 535 N. Dearborn St., Chicago, Illinois. Pamphlets of excellent quality, available for 50¢ each. About 50 pages each.

Facts Aren't Enough. A discussion of the physical and emotional aspects of sex, addressed to those who have responsibilities for the education of children and youth.

Finding Yourself. Answers many questions of boys and girls of junior high age, presenting the basis for a sound understanding of sex.

* = Specially recommended

141

Approaching Adulthood. For young people from 16 to 20 years of age. A straightforward discussion of sound facts leading to healthy attitudes toward sex and marriage.

AMERICAN SOCIAL HEALTH ASSOCIATION. 1790 Broadway, New York, New York 10019.

Attaining Manhood, by Corner. $1.50.

Attaining Womanhood, by Corner. $1.50. Two books for boys and girls of high school age. Scientific accounts of sex and human reproduction.

Emotional Problems of Growing Up, by English and Finch. 60¢. Suggests ways to help teen-agers adjust to adult life.

Facts of Life and Love for Teenagers, by Evelyn Duvall. $3.50. Contains concrete situations any young person may wonder about and come up against. Answers most questions simply and directly. A basic text for adults and their teen-agers. Reprinted as a Popular Library paperback for 35¢.

Know Your Daughter and *Know Your Son.* Two pamphlets, 25¢ each, for parents to discuss with girls and boys, 10 to 14 years of age.

New Patterns in Sex Teaching, by Strain. An extensive manual for study group leaders who are interested in sex education. $2.75.

New Ways in Sex Education, by Baruch. $4.75. A guide for parents and teachers.

Understanding Sex, by Kirkendall. 50¢. Basic facts about physical development, boy-girl relationships, and the importance of mature attitudes toward sex. Available through American Health Association or through the publisher, with direct orders in quantity receiving reduced rates.

Inquiries about quantity rates: Science Research Associates, 57 W. Grand Ave., Chicago 10, Illinois.

The publications listed above are directly available from the Association; not all are published by the group, and are often available elsewhere as well.

CHILD STUDY ASSOCIATION OF AMERICA, INC. 9 East 89th St., New York, New York, 10028.

When Children Ask about Sex. 40¢. A handbook of how, when and how much to tell about sex at various age levels.

FAMILY LIFE PUBLICATIONS, INC. Box 6725, College Station, Durham, North Carolina.

*Human Growth, by Beck. Harcourt, Brace & Co. This book promotes good attitudes toward sex as it teaches the older child and adolescent how boys and girls grow up. Explains physical changes during adolescence and their meaning for adult life. Companion to the film "Human Growth," used extensively by junior high schools. $2.75.

For Teenagers Only, by Richardson. $2.95. Addressed in non-authoritarian language to young people aged 14 to 17 who long to get married "right now."

*The Stork Didn't Bring You, by Pemberton. $2.95. Sex education for teenagers. Answers questions young people are too shy to ask. Recommended by Parents Magazine and the National Council of the YMCA.

OTHER PUBLICATIONS

Sex Guidance for your Child, ed. Helen I. Driver. Monona Publications, P.O. Box 3222, Madison 4, Wisconsin. $4.50. Four distinguished authors deal with problems of child-rearing and sex guidance for children. Definite answers are given to questions about sex information, attitudes and behavior of children which pertain to sex.

Love and the Facts of Life, by Evelyn Millis Duvall. Association Press, 291 Broadway, New York 7, New York. 1963. $4.95. The new Duvall book is a replacement for the older *Facts of Life and Love for Teenagers*, and may be the finest publication available for high school youth on the subject. A *must* for the parish library if it is used generally by the congregation. Reproduction, emotional factors, dating, petting, marriage, popularity—all discussed fully and in a dignified and understandable manner. May be available in paperback by 1965.

Sex Attitudes in the Home, by Ralph G. Eckert. Association Press (see last entry above), $3.50. Also available as a Popular Library paperback at 35¢. A frank, dignified discussion, documented by examples of common situations, showing how the sex values of young people are influenced by home attitudes in general. An important book for parents. Should be considered for distribution to parents if a Family Life Education course is taken up in the Parish.

FILMS

Boy to Man. Color. 16 minutes. 1961. An outstanding, perhaps the best film on the development of adolescent boys. Explains physical change such as growth of body hair, change of voice, genital and pituitary development; discusses masturbation, differences in growth patterns, development of girls. Diagrammatic portrayals of functions of reproductive organs in boys and girls. Winner of bronze medal, Venice Film Festival. Suitable for Junior High boys, and mixed groups of Senior High boys and girls. A guide is available from the producer, Churchill Films, Suite 1520, 6671 Sunset Blvd., Los Angeles 28, California.

Human Growth. Color. 20 minutes. 1948. Generally partments. Produced by the E. C. Brown Trust, University of Oregon. Excellent resource on reproduction and puberty changes, suitable for grades 6–9, boys and girls. Presented in an instructional atmosphere (a 7th grade classroom). Menstruation, body changes, hair growth, genital development all discussed plainly. A filmstrip, textbook are also available for advisors. A take-home pamphlet is also used for distribution with showing of the film: *The Gift of Life,* Health Education Service, P.O. Box 7283, Albany, New York 12224. Approved by Roman Catholic, Protestant and Jewish leaders.

Human Reproduction. Black and White. 23 minutes. 1948. Originally produced for college-level and adults. McGraw-Hill film, available generally. The most complete, albeit dated, film on reproduction. Very thorough coverage of male and female development, shown by diagrams and models. Major resource for groups of parents, good for High School, mature for Junior High. Discusses: anatomy, embryology, body mechanics of the delivery process. Film-strip also available. This film is the one recommended in the Seabury Press book *Fit to be Tied* by Batten and Mc-Lean.

Films on menstruation for girls: *The Story of Menstruation, Molly Grows Up* and *Confidence Because—You Understand Menstruation* (filmstrip). These are often available through state film libraries and from school districts. Usually presented to 6th, 7th and 8th grade girls, although some schools use them in fifth grade. Boys also are shown these films separately. Pamphlets prepared commercially by several manufacturers are available for free distribution to girls. Watch what your school districts are doing about showing these films: many are doing so, and it is not necessary to repeat their efforts.

MIXED MARRIAGES

One Marriage Two Faiths, by James H. S. Bossard and Eleanor Stoker Boll. New York, Ronald Press Co., 1957.

If You Marry Outside Your Faith, by James A. Pike, Harper Row, New York, New York 1962. (Available in both hard cover and paper-back editions)

ALCOHOL AND SEX

Alcoholics Anonymous, 2nd Ed. 1955. Published by Alcoholics Anonymous Pub. Inc., New York. Basic sourcebook for the inquirer who seeks to understand the phenomenon and social impact of alcoholism and other problem drinking.

Marty Mann's Primer on Alcoholism, 1958. Holt, Rinehart & Winston Co., Inc., New York. Another basic guide to the phenomenon of alcoholism and its social consequences.

The National Council on Alcoholism, Inc., 2 East 103rd Street, New York, New York 10029. Provides specific pamphlets and other guidance about teen-agers and alcohol upon request.